ABOUT THE AUTHOR

Tim Vincent, leading headhunter and CEO of global recruitment specialist Rembrandt Consultants Ltd, reveals the confidential tools, coaching and guidance that have helped them ensure that their candidates receive rave reviews from every interview.

Also author of *Shore Raker*, a career perspective parable published for Kindle in 2012, Tim remains hands-on at the helm of Rembrandt where he personally handles some of the world's most challenging recruitment assignments.

TIM VINCENT

→ NAIL THAT INTERVIEW

ANSWER
TOUGH QUESTIONS

MAKE THE
BEST IMPRESSION

AND
GET THE JOB

Vermilion
LONDON

1 3 5 7 9 10 8 6 4 2

Published in 2013 by Vermilion, an imprint of Ebury Publishing
Ebury Publishing is a Random House Group company

The Random House Group Limited Reg. No. 954009
Addresses for companies within the Random House Group can be found at
www.randomhouse.co.uk

A CIP catalogue record for this book is available from the British Library

The Random House Group Limited supports The Forest Stewardship Council®
(FSC®), the leading international forest-certification organisation. Our books
carrying the FSC label are printed on FSC®-certified paper. FSC is the only
forest-certification scheme supported by the leading environmental organisations,
including Greenpeace. Our paper procurement policy can be found at
www.randomhouse.co.uk/environment

Designed and set by seagulls.net

Printed and bound in Great Britain by Clays Ltd, St Ives PLC

ISBN 9780091948214

Copies are available at special rates for bulk orders.
Contact the sales development team on 020 7840 8487 for more information

To buy books by your favourite authors and register for offers, visit
www.randomhouse.co.uk

CONTENTS

For Kate, Mia, Evie and Angus

YOUR INTERVIEW, YOUR CAREER

Welcome to a whole new look at job interviews.

The interview is a misunderstood meeting. And yes, although you might not have thought of it in this way before, the interview is indeed a meeting. A business meeting, to be more precise, in which both parties are essentially trying to decide whether or not they want to work together.

> *Interviewer:* Do I buy this candidate?
> *Candidate:* Do I buy this job?

'Buy' might be an unfamiliar word to you in this context, but it's a word that you will come to know well as you work through this book. For *buy* you can, if you prefer, read *choose* or *select*. Making good buying decisions requires skill and perhaps a little luck, but when it comes to significant decisions such as which career path to buy then your skills ought to be as sharp as possible so that you don't rely on being lucky. Your career path is one you only get to walk once. So try to make sure the route you take is the right one.

This book cuts through some of the more commonly held misconceptions about the interview and gives you a clear process to follow that will help ensure you are prepared to give of your very best every time you walk into an interview and take the candidate's chair.

I'm a headhunter. I search out exceptional talent. Over some 16 years of recruiting I have been asked to find candidates, up and down the seniority ladder, across industry sectors, from all around the globe. Once a candidate has been successfully selected for a role, I help them decide whether or not to accept the job offer and join our clients' businesses.

All of the candidates we submit on shortlists end up representing themselves and our company at interviews. Without exception, these candidates tend to believe they interview either 'very well', 'pretty well' or at least 'okay', whereas unfortunately we have learnt the hard way that however good they are at their day job, the majority are, in fact, hopeless when it comes to selling themselves in interviews.

If, following the interview, our client doesn't hire our candidate then we don't get our placement fee. So I have become fascinated by interviews and what it takes to be successful at them. In this book I have pulled together all that I have learnt and set out the now well-proven, 10-step process my colleagues and I have developed to help ensure our candidates *nail* interviews for themselves and for us.

Nail That Interview will help you do exactly what the book title says. Take these 10 steps one at a time to ensure you are thoroughly prepared, rehearsed and poised to nail *any* job interview. Whether you are a first-timer, expert veteran, junior intern or senior board member, these steps are equally effective.

IT'S YOUR MEETING

You have *more* than an equal responsibility to make the interview a worthwhile and successful meeting. Note I stress the word 'more'. You, the candidate, are in charge of this meeting. It is *your* meeting. At stake is *your* career. Potentially several years of your life ride on what you invest in this interview. On the other hand, the person interviewing you simply has one empty seat and possibly three to ten candidates. I don't care how senior a person is required to fill the position – cleaner to CEO/president, this meeting belongs to the candidate *not* the interviewer.

Ask yourself the following question:

What has to happen for the job I am interviewing for to serve as a sturdy rung on the stepladder to my dream career?

My aim is to help you be honest first with yourself and then with others so that the interview stands a better than average chance of taking you where you want to go.

IT'S ALL ABOUT ATTITUDE

Good interviewers these days are trying to gauge the candidates' *attitude* because having the 'right attitude' is commonly perceived as the single most important criterion required for success.

In the past I presume you might well have prepared for interviews with a few obvious moves:

- Clean shoes
- Buy new suit
- Get hair done
- Bone up on interviewer
- Arrive early
- Remember to shake hand firmly

Additionally, if you are like many of my candidates, you will have searched the Internet for examples of common interview questions and how best to answer them. Here are some examples of questions and suggested responses that you'll readily find online for free:

Q. Do you make mistakes?
A. (Be honest.) Yes, of course, on occasions, but I obviously try not to, and I always try to correct them and learn from them.

Q. How do you plan and organise your work?
A. Planning and writing a plan is very important. I think how best to do things before I do them. If it's unknown territory I'd take advice, learn from previous examples – why reinvent the wheel? I always

prioritise, I manage my time and I understand the difference between urgent and important. For very complex projects I'd produce quite a detailed schedule and plan review stages. I even plan time slots for activities that aren't in themselves organised, like thinking time and being creative, solving problems, etc.

Q. What type of people do you get on with most/least?
A. Generally I get on with everyone. I respond most to genuine, positive, honest people. (If pressed as to people you don't get on with, say that you respect people for their differences and seek to understand them, rather than seeing differences to be a reason for conflict or difficulty.)

So now we know where all the rubbish that the average candidate reels off comes from. Honestly … what a waste of everyone's time!

If you are ever interviewed by someone who hires you just because you gave a few snappy answers (better than those above I assume) at an interview – turn the job down. They are idiots! What do you think pre-rehearsed, one-size-fits-all answers tell an interviewer about your attitude?

By giving you the proven principles and coaching you to apply them, you won't need to surf the Web to find answers to stock interview questions. Rather you will have a structure around which the entire relationship between you and the interviewer is built.

CAREER CATALYST

In completing the 10 steps you will come to realise that the job interview, rather than being a daunting test or scary audition, can be a significant and powerful catalyst for your evolving career.

More than how to pass smoothly through the interview doorway, you will learn how to use the interview to build and develop your career into what *you* want it to be. The preparation for the interview and the meeting itself can, when well executed, reveal and realise your (perhaps as yet unknown) career dream.

The actual job for which the interview was arranged in the first place should not be the sole basis and focus of the meeting. In fact the job behind the interview might in this context be seen as a *distraction* from the broader possibilities. Adopting this attitude encourages you to actively seek out and explore the wider career opportunities through the interview doorway. Possibilities will be revealed that you hadn't dreamt of. You will see how to realise them and set the wheels in motion to actually achieve them.

POSTMAN TO CEO

Provided you, the candidate, arrive well prepared and with the right attitude, the interview for *any* job can be used to launch you on a trajectory towards *any* career target. For example, the trainee internal postman can become CEO of a Fortune 500 company. Manny Fontenla-Novoa started out in the post room of a travel business and rose to take the helm at Thomas Cook, a globally recognised brand that he led with great skill. When Manny interviewed for that postie job do you think he took the right attitude with him?

Something is attracting you to go for another job and you think the interview stands in your way as an obstacle. You would like to get to the opportunity beyond. So the interview represents some form of career stepping stone for you.

I don't think the interview stands in your way. On the contrary, I see the interview as your opportunity to explore your dream career with the selected representative of the shareholders/owners of the company you are considering working with.

Preparing for the interview is the simple and exciting first step to realising your dream career. This book will show you how to harness your knowledge and understanding so that you can drive your career forward in exciting ways.

YOU HAVE TO HAMMER THE NAIL HOME

So the good news is that, when *nailed*, the interview can be *hugely* effective. Indeed it can be one of *the* most effective business meetings you ever attend.

The bad news is that you, the candidate, have to wield the hammer that hits the nail all by yourself because the traditional interview is, root and branch, designed to fail the lofty objectives set for it. It sits nestled as a process point, a singular stage within what will likely be a broad candidate selection process. As the candidate you are being considered for a role you probably know little about, by people who likely know absolutely nothing about you, in a meeting that asks that both parties make the call to go/no go based on whatever they *feel* following this face-to-face session.

The interview meeting is indeed unlikely to be effective. In fact, it is very likely to be dangerously ineffective at what it is intended for. Interviews (or more specifically, 60-minute meetings designed to select candidates for specified roles on the one hand, and for aspiring careerists to select their next career platform on the other) happen in the many millions worldwide every day and they are, for the most part, appallingly conducted by both interviewer and candidate.

Not any more. You the candidate can use the 10 steps outlined here to make sure your interview is well conducted, meaningful and fruitful. Pick up the hammer and get ready to swing.

LET'S NAIL IT

Like any good meeting, whether business or otherwise, you should go into the interview with clear objectives. These are:

1. To answer the question: 'Do I want the job?'
2. To persuade the interviewer to want you for the job.
3. To clarify and agree on the next steps – how does this process lead to an offer?

To help ensure that you meet these objectives and indeed nail that interview, you are going to take 10 simple steps one at a time.

THE 10 STEPS

Step 1. **Write your CV**
Step 2. **Reveal your career frame**
Step 3. **Reveal your core**
Step 4. **Plot your career trajectory**
Step 5. **Capture your USPs***
Step 6. **Draft your stories**
Step 7. **Research the role**
Step 8. **Ready your answers**
Step 9. **Nail your questions**
Step 10. **Practice**

* Unique selling points.

USING THIS BOOK

Before we dive in, here are three pointers that will help you nail it first time!

KEEP A JOURNAL

This journal is for your thoughts, reflections on and specific responses to each of the 10 steps. This will help ensure you retain everything for future reference because each time an interview comes around you will need to remind yourself, after all. (My instructions on using the journal are given for a handwritten notebook, but you can use an electronic format; whatever you feel most comfortable with.)

I will indicate where you need to use your journal with the following symbol: 📖

READ THE INSTRUCTION MANUAL

Are you the kind of person who reads instruction manuals or, like me, do you prefer to be hands-on and figure stuff out as you go along?

Most of us have a tendency to simply get on with things and are too impatient to bother. We do miss something here. Usually it will be relatively minor but in some cases we can damage an appliance or, worst-case scenario, injure ourselves if we don't read and follow the instructions.

I recall the tale one candidate related of how his mate had bought a garden zip wire for his children and asked him to help set it up. He went round to his friend's house and found the zip wire assembled: all they had to do was run the wire between the selected trees. In his haste his mate had mislaid the instructions. No bother, it couldn't be that difficult. Could it?

To cut a long story short, an eight-year-old girl (the friend's daughter) ended up travelling at speed between the two trees and then beyond them some way distant into an adjacent field. Fortunately, she only sustained a few bruises.

Her father and his mate looked at each other with expressions that were a mixture of relief and shock. They had taken a stupid risk, but had got away with it on this occasion.

And the moral of this story? Simply that here in your hands you have an instruction manual for the interview meeting. Don't be tempted to skim it or skip over the parts you think you already know. Your career zip wire can fling you off into all sorts of weird and wonderful places. It's better to be in control. Read your instruction manual, this book, with care to ensure you use these meetings to best effect.

THE RIGHT PACE

Having said this, it might not be possible for you to carefully work your way through this book as it depends when your next interview is. If you don't have that much time it's important that you focus on the priorities and these will vary depending on the amount of time you have available. The box below will help you set the right pace for your preparation.

When is your next interview?	My recommendations and advice on how to use this book to the best effect
Not sure. At the moment I have no interview planned. I'm interested in career development and how I can make sure I am ready.	Perfect. Not only do you get to absorb the 10 steps at your leisure, you also get to play with the material in a variety of different settings before your next important interview encounter. However, to help ensure you really do get to grips with the techniques and principles, I recommend that you pretend that you have an interview in about 30 days' time. This will give your preparation some impetus and a sense of importance that will, to some extent, mirror what you will feel when you have a real interview looming.
In more than 10 days' time.	Schedule some personal time in your diary every day (a minimum of one hour per day) until the day before your interview. Over the time you have available, read the whole book, work through the 10 steps and try to ensure you have completed your journal. Ideally you should leave yourself four days to rehearse using Step 10 as your guide, so build this into your schedule. Monitor your progress and pace to ensure you don't overrun.
8–10 days' time.	Schedule some personal time in your diary every day (a minimum of two hours per day) until the day before your interview. Read the book through, but if you have already shared your CV with the interviewer (as it's likely that you will have by this point) I recommend a skim read of Step 1, but don't complete it, just move straight to Step 2. Monitor your pace carefully. You should aim to leave yourself two days as opposed to the luxury of four for rehearsal and practice.

When is your next interview?	My recommendations and advice on how to use this book to the best effect	
6–7 days' time.	As above but make your journal less of a priority to enable you to focus on the production of Prompt Sheets #1 (see page 78) and #2 (see page 139). Your reading of the whole book should still be timed to allow you two days to refine and rehearse the use of the prompt sheets.	
5 days' time.	As above but schedule only one day for rehearsal.	
4 days' time.	Go straight to Step 5 and aim to read through to the end of Step 9 in a day. Then follow the advice below for the final three days before your interview.	
3 days' time.	Provided you accept that this meeting will be more for experience and practice then leave it in place, but if you really want the role then I recommend you ask for a postponement. Use the line: 'I have looked into my preparedness and realised that in order to do the meeting justice I need to turn up with the right questions for you as this is a two-way exchange. How is your diary ten days from now?' If this fails or you want to go ahead and practise then accept that you aren't going to nail the interview but you'll give it your best shot in the time available.	1. Go straight to Step 5 and read through all the subsequent steps paying particular attention to Step 6 to draft your stories and the question structure in Step 9, both of which yield critical prompt sheets you need for your interview pack. 2. Look up the bio of the person you are meeting. Print it off. 3. Research the company in detail. Find the latest information, news articles and announcements. Look over the job specification if you have one. Consider the gaps between you and the role requirements.

When is your next interview?	My recommendations and advice on how to use this book to the best effect	
1 or 2 days' time.		As above but: a. Skip some of the detail in Point 3. Go for a skim here. b. Only aim for five questions and two stories.
Tomorrow.		Ask for a postponement to allow you more time to prepare for what is a very important meeting. Failing this: a. Take the rest of today off if possible. b. Only aim for three questions and one story.

If the timing of your next interview doesn't allow you to go through the book in detail, do find the time once the interview is over. Allow yourself the space to reflect on some of the finer points of your career; this is the sort of thinking that simply doesn't usually surface through the noise of your busy life.

I am pleased to reassure you that whether you're looking for a job, moving jobs, hoping to rekindle enthusiasm, change career tack or simply seek greater progression in your current career – and whenever you are next due to be interviewed – *Nail That Interview* is the right place for you to begin. This book will help you turn the interview from a scary firewall into an open doorway to your dream career.

Whatever you have in mind – nail it!

STEP 1: WRITE YOUR CV

'Thank you for coming along this afternoon. Would you mind beginning with a little bit about yourself? Just take me through the highlights. You know. Tell me who you are.'

Whoa! If there was a list of challenging interview questions this one would be right up there. It usually comes early in the meeting at a time when you are hoping to be given a slightly easier ride. It might well be asked by a senior manager who has only just received your curriculum vitae (CV) from their PA and is buying time to glance through your vitals while they figure out a more interesting question or two.

This type of opening question is commonly used but it is a challenge for the candidate. It's a great place for us to start because:

1. It is a blunt reminder of the sort of bizarre meeting you are going into.
2. It reveals a great deal about the interviewer and you will learn here how to gain strong control over the meeting from this type of opening question.
3. It is actually a great question to use on yourself to help get you in the right frame of mind as we begin.

The third point listed above is the most important. At an interview you are selling *you*. You are the product. You are on the shelf. Just you. So we had better begin by understanding a little about you. A lot about you in fact. We need to get to know you really well so that we can sell you.

We are going to start to prepare for the interview where career advisers, headhunters and prospective employers begin with most candidates – the CV.

THE CV MINDSET

Before diving into the CV itself we first need to look at who you *really* are, and do so in the right frame of mind. Understanding who you are is important in this context because it's the basis of what you're going to put in your CV and what goes into your CV ought to be an accurate reflection of reality.

Honest self-analysis can be tricky. I usually find candidates are inclined to be a combination of modest and bashful; however, it is critical that you are candid with yourself. This is not the time to hide your light under a bushel, nor is it helpful to view yourself through rose-tinted glasses.

Following are the three points I find best help those I coach to get into the right mindset before putting together their CV.

1. BE YOUR OWN HERO

We often reference others as we place ourselves in the spotlight. We look to extraordinary individuals for inspiration, from the extremely successful in our immediate vicinity, such as friends, family or work colleagues, to global icons.

Our culture and the media eulogise the achievements of these global icons, which might suggest that we should strive to be just like them. Apparently, not only can we learn from what they have achieved and how they have achieved it, but, by implication, we can model our own career and achievements around theirs.

Possibly, for the truly remarkable among us, we can. But a far more practical approach would be to consider the wise reflection offered by creative strategist, consultant and writer Royale Scuderi:

Don't measure yourself against other people, measure yourself against your own yardstick.

Hero worship and striving to be like others is seldom of real use, whether the hero is someone famous or someone a little closer to home who has skills or qualities that you admire. Being inspired by extraordinary people is certainly good and the human spirit can achieve amazing things, but don't let these lofty goals distract you from setting realistic ones for yourself. Every journey is one step after another and it's your steps that are important, not trying to live up to the journeys of others.

2. PATS ON THE BACK AND SETBACKS

Too often we don't take the time to congratulate ourselves when we are doing things right. So pat yourself on the back for one or two of your better decisions.

At the same time, acknowledge the setbacks you have suffered that have informed your wisdom. Facing failures is a cornerstone of great success. Every setback in life provides another stone for your personal foundation. I take candidates through a career-reflection stage that draws out the mishaps and hiccups along the way, as well as the successes and high points. We can usually line up their setbacks like a row of stones that points to what they have become. Here are two examples of setbacks from two different candidates:

SALES MANAGER
A sales manager missed his budget by a huge margin and learnt from this never to accept an unrealistic budget but to ensure he pushed back until the numbers were rooted in reality at the outset. Since this setback he has not fallen short of his budget and has become known as the benchmark for overachievement.

SENIOR DATABASE ENGINEER
The engineer delegated a small task to a friend who was unemployed and learnt that mixing business with personal relationships can cause you to relax normally rigid and important standards. The subsequent

mess was one that took two weekends and many late evenings to unwind. He considered he had been lucky – the whole project had been threatened. He raised the bar instead of lowering it for any friends he engaged subsequently.

Neither of them could have paid for better lessons than these. Both of them, when reflecting, realised just how critical these incidents were to forming the behaviour that earned them their subsequent success.

Sprinkled among major examples such as these are the many smaller failings experienced by all career-minded people who set out to try and succeed, but they know and understand that such setbacks go to make up the rungs they will use to climb their career ladder.

3. DEFINE SUCCESS IN YOUR OWN TERMS

Consider the story of James, who is a candidate I coached out of making a very poor fist of a key review meeting he was preparing for. As is so often the case, his career setbacks were significant and painful for him.

James had joined the company in its infancy and played a key role in driving growth over his seven years' tenure with them. He had regularly been overlooked for promotion up the ranks as his contribution to front-line sales was considered too critical. He had become negative towards the company and his senior management team, having seen too many people join on more generous remuneration packages than his own. In his view these new recruits didn't have his ability and experience. When we met for this particular coaching session he was scheduled to see his line manager the following day and in his words: 'If he doesn't promote me and raise my pay in line with my peers I am walking!'

We needed to begin by redefining what a successful outcome for this meeting would be or it was pretty clear to me that he would be 'walking'!

It turned out that he was earning very well since his bonuses were linked to sales and he was succeeding. It also transpired that he loved selling and had no particular aspirations to do the administrative side of man-management. Furthermore, he had loved being recognised on stage at the global conference in the previous quarter.

With some further digging we managed to uncover what was at the root of his dissatisfaction. He told me that his best friend didn't recognise any of the above factors as positives; rather he held the narrow view that the de facto measures of success are title and basic pay. This guy nagged him to continually press for more and when he failed to get it he blamed firstly the employer for not recognising him fairly and secondly his friend for failing to get his just desserts.

It is easy to see how he might be drawn into defining success on terms that were defined by:

- His best friend, who apparently held a narrow view of progress measures
- The managers, who had bigger titles, bigger pay cheques, but very different roles

His terms needed to be his own. Once I had coached him to recognise this we worked together to prepare him for the meeting and he went in with a very different agenda:

- Expand territory
- Adopt vacant accounts
- Negotiate stock bundle for over-target performance
- Recognition as 'senior pursuit lead' for Central Europe

All of which he secured. In the subsequent 12-month period he more than doubled his income to record levels. Much of it he was now receiving as stock options that it turns out were destined for significant heights.

Now, in his view, he is a success. I don't know how his best friend feels and I honestly don't care!

Making success something you *expect* for yourself will be greatly helped if you follow three simple guidelines:

I. START SMALL

If you are a couch potato today, you would be ill-advised to run a marathon tomorrow, because even if you were to succeed you would be putting your health at risk. Begin by making improvements and enhancements that are reassuringly achievable, before stretching yourself further. For example, you might get up 10 minutes earlier tomorrow, do five press-ups and eat a yogurt. The next day add a short stroll, and so on. By taking a series of progressive steps people complete triathlons or run marathons. Apply the same principles to your career aspirations. By all means go for big, lofty goals, but make sure you allow yourself lots of little success checkpoints en route. As the saying goes, 'An inch is a cinch. A yard is hard.'

2. WELCOME SETBACKS

Accept that setbacks, however large, are a part of attempting to further yourself. They are the means by which you gather the necessary stones to build your personal foundation for success. Be very conscious of this at the start and you will welcome failure as a characteristic of looming success. You will no longer be among the many who give up when the going gets a little tougher than they had imagined in their daydreams.

When you imagine success allow yourself to consider the obstacles you are likely to encounter and see yourself handling each in turn. Again you are working to *your* terms here. To use the couch-potato analogy again, your personal terms should acknowledge that you first need to adjust your attitude and form some new habits before taking on a rigorous fitness-training programme.

3. CELEBRATE SUCCESS

While recognising successes as milestones to your broader progress they also act as reassurances. Do celebrate each successful achievement and do it with as much energy as you can. Be your own biggest fan. We fall too readily into the habit of dwelling on the negatives when actually positives abound.

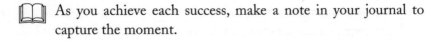 As you achieve each success, make a note in your journal to capture the moment.

THE CV AS A TOOL

I am frequently asked by candidates: 'Do I need to redo my CV if I already have one?' The answer to this question is yes. Drawing up your CV is the critical first step to ensure that you are working from a solid foundation from the outset. But as you may have grasped, the action of putting together your CV is actually valuable on many levels. Initially I recommend you approach your CV as a self-coaching tool and ultimately the end product becomes one of the keys that opens the door to the interview and indeed furnishes the interviewer with their briefing notes for the meeting.

The CV, when well structured, should act as a useful tool in three areas to:

- **Self-coach**: Understanding how you arrived where you are; this is the career management summary to date for yourself.
- **Direct**: Thinking about your key skills, experience and other talents; picking out the strong threads and achievements to date will help direct your career planning.
- **Communicate**: Providing a proven, well-established way of getting your profile to decision-makers; this is the traditional role of the CV as a sales support document (remember, the CV is presenting you). A hiring manager should be able to grasp quickly your value to their team.

What job you are interviewing for and at which organisation does not matter at this stage. Whether internal or external our preparation approach will be just the same and the CV just as valuable.

- **Internal move**: An internal move should be treated no differently to an external one. Essentially, you are still moving from one employer to another as usually your reporting line changes. However minor this change might be, you should prepare to be screened for the new role as thoroughly as if you were being hired from outside the business. Don't make the mistake of assuming that the new line managers who are going to be looking at your CV have access to all of the documentation on you or that they know you well through contact with other colleagues or perhaps because you've socialised with them. Assume the reverse and you will probably be closer to the truth.

- **External move**: When applying to a new organisation (or perhaps for your first job) the CV is the essential headline summary that helps support your case to join the company. It acts as the teaser that gets you an interview.

WE BUY ATTITUDE

This is a timely reminder of the importance of attitude and the need to project yours positively throughout the process – beginning with your CV.

When a headhunter is trying to tease out all of the attributes our client is looking for in an ideal candidate we use questions such as:

- What are the key behaviour traits that the ideal candidate would exhibit?
- How will you know that you have found the right candidate?
- When you interview, what sort of specific aspects do you like to focus on?
- What three headline successes would an ideal individual have achieved within their first 12 months working for you in this role?

There is, however, one question that we have always found particularly useful in these assignment briefings:

'When all is said and done, what one word do you feel best describes the person you want to hire for this role?'

Sixteen years ago the most common answer we got in response was:

Experienced

We can logically assess experience. It has highly measurable aspects that are easily verified. It is indeed reassuring to know that a candidate has already proven they can do what you want them to do.

Today the most common answer to this question is very different. In actual fact, the answer is now usually one of these three:

Attitude – Presence – Substance

These attributes are not easy to measure and assess but projecting positive attitude through your CV should be much easier when you use the template (see pages 21–22). These qualities are also more difficult for the candidate to manipulate since they get a lot closer to the real you, the inner self if you like.

It is not the case that our clients have stopped looking for experience. Rather that it has simply dropped down the criteria ranking. We sense they are saying to us: 'Find me a person that I can relate to and be impressed by. Then let's make sure they have the other stuff.'

We have found that candidates who demonstrate the right attitude are people who seem to have a very good handle on who they are. Hopefully, once you have drawn up your CV you are somewhat closer to this clarity yourself. For sure you will have a sharper insight that in turn will help you project enhanced attitude, presence and substance when the topic is you! First impressions really do count and in many cases your CV will land ahead of you. Nail it!

THE CV TEMPLATE

The CV is not supposed to be a complete history of you. It should be designed as a summary, focusing on the key points about you. You are the product and we need to big you up. The content and layout should ideally make it easy for the reader to glance through your CV and gain a good insight into your skills, experience and background. If it goes beyond two A4 pages, it's too long. The temptation to oversell yourself is huge. When you're concerned about securing an interview, you may well feel compelled to go to substantial lengths to justify why you deserve the job. Unfortunately, it's very difficult to do that to any useful or reliable extent on your CV.

The good news is that there is a well-proven, tested and effective CV template. The CV samples that follow (see pages 25–31) meet a set of simple yet critical guidelines.

1. Font choice is a matter of taste, but there is a lot to be said for the readability of Times New Roman. I recommend a point size of 12, but whatever you do don't use anything less than 10.
2. Your name is at the top in a large, bold font. There is absolutely no need for the title 'Curriculum Vitae'.
3. What you are at your professional core is captured succinctly and compellingly without any fluff immediately beneath your name. This is the headline description of what you are professionally.
4. What you want is stated next. To help affirm that you aspire to something that the reader can understand and probably assist with.
5. Next your professional career chronology in reverse order so the most recent role is listed first. Critically, the relevant dates are in the left margin to enable a scan to any point in your history without risking confusion over when you did it and for how long. This section has to be kept extremely simple and yet content rich.
6. Education and the remainder are towards the tail end as they are usually not a priority and are of less interest to the reader.

WHAT YOU SHOULDN'T INCLUDE IN YOUR CV

Just as important as what is included in your CV, is what you leave out. Please resist the urge to add anything 'clever' to your CV. Specifically avoid:

- Photos
- Generic covering letter

- Appendices
- Payslips
- References
- Diagrams
- Logos

I still get new and creative angles on the CV sent through to me, though none, I admit, as creative as the award winners you will find published each year by Business Insider. Try searching online for 'insanely creative resumes'. Here you will find among others:

- A CV designed to look like a Facebook page (complete with complimentary wall comments).
- One set out like a Google page where the search was 'Creative+Excellent Designer'.
- A CV sewn into cloth by a graphic designer who was a keen sewer.

Creative slants such as these on the traditional career summary are indeed entertaining and compelling. These particularly creative examples did actually help the respective candidates get interviews and indeed land jobs, but I don't think they needed to go to these extremes. Too much effort and emphasis placed on the CV as a sales instrument runs the risk of giving the impression that the candidate behind the CV has to dress themselves up because they might lack the core quality that should speak for itself.

That said, if you are indeed going for a job as a clothing designer at a funky clothing company you might go so far as to make your sewn CV part of your proposition because there are exceptions to my principles and guidelines; some insanely creative jobs do indeed justify insanely creative CVs to win an invitation to an interview in the first instance. They are the rare exception and in my view the CV is not the right medium for expressing your creative flair. Please resist the temptation to indulge your talents here.

At the other end of the scale are those CVs we receive that are simply poor because they are:

- Too long
- Too short
- Unstructured or badly structured
- Full of spelling errors and typos
- Full of employment gaps that are not explained
- Incomplete and miss out an employer altogether that is shown elsewhere (e.g. on LinkedIn)
- Not consistent in style and use of font

Accuracy is crucial so check each detail carefully and make sure there are no gaps or inconsistencies. Ask someone who knows you well to read through this core content to ensure it is spot on.

If you follow these guidelines your CV will be laid out in the correct order. It will have all of the information that a prospective employer or recruiter needs to see and it won't have any extraneous detail or sales puff. Simply put, this template works.

Example 1 (opposite) is the CV of a recent graduate; Example 2 (see page 28) is for a more senior level executive. What I'm showing you here is that the template is identical for candidates who are at completely different ends of their careers. Don't be put off if the content doesn't relate closely to your career, rather notice the application of the template and guidelines I have set out.

Follow the template and draw up your CV. Print a copy off and keep it in the front of your journal.

CV EXAMPLE I

James Vino

117b Etherly Road, London, E18 1QJ, England
tel: 09768 473871 (M), 0608 874 281 (H), email: jvino33@yap.co.uk

A POSTGRADUATE with significant experience in sales, leadership, coaching and presenting. A qualified coach of martial arts. An academic foundation in Classics and International Relations.

OBJECTIVE: A challenging opportunity requiring the application of a broad range of skills and knowledge with a particular interest in international travel in the short–medium term.

Dec 2008–date	***Mac Zone* Magazine, Future Publishing, Freelance Writer**

- Wrote numerous video-game reviews as well as other articles and features that were published in several issues in 2009
- Also involved with brainstorming ideas for the magazine, one of which became a recurring feature that was highly rated in reader feedback sessions

Nov 2008	***The Chronicle and Echo* Newspaper, Research Assistant**

- Provided administrative support to the news desk and wrote news reports of varying length. Shadowed a number of correspondents and assisted with vox pop surveys and interviews with local politicians
- Recognised by the editor as 'particularly determined and adept at impartiality in his research and information gathering'

June–Sept 2007	**Richards No.1 Bar, Nottsborough, Bar Associate**

- Managed the main bar area for a local branch of a major chain of public houses. Completed three initial modules of the in-house management-training programme with distinction
- Increased up-sell by 18% and reduced losses through fraud, breakages and spillage by over 60% during my tenure. Rated as 'Future Star' by Regional Head

June–Sept 2004   **Ecco Shoes, Nottsborough, Sales Assistant**
                        • Rapidly rose to assume responsibility for key shift
                          leadership
Aug 2003– July 2006   **Cargin Moss Black Belt Academy, Martial Arts
                        Coaching Assistant**
                        • Delivered 45-minute tae kwon do lessons to
                          children aged from 5 to 13. The classes generally
                          consisted of 30 to 40 children. A typical lesson
                          would involve a combination of warm-up drills,
                          self-defence techniques, fitness exercises and
                          training for competitions
                        • Responsible for helping prepare lesson plans
                          for each session, ensuring that all the necessary
                          components were included to make the classes as
                          beneficial and safe as possible for the students
                        • Many students still reach out to me for pointers in
                          their further development

OTHER RECENT ACHIEVEMENTS AND ACTIVITIES

Jan–June 2009   ***The Arts and Culture Show*, University Radio
                        Nottsborough, Co-presenter**
                        • Researched, planned and presented a weekly
                          programme that covered a variety of topics
                          including local events in Nottsborough, film,
                          theatre and current affairs
                        • Responsible for organising and hosting weekly
                          planning meetings where we would assign
                          individual topics and discuss ways of improving the
                          show
Sept 2008–May 2009   ***Impact* Magazine, Contributor**
                        • Regularly wrote film reviews for Nottsborough
                          University's student magazine

EDUCATION / QUALIFICATIONS

2009–2010   **MA International Security and Terrorism (Distinction Expected), University of Nottsborough**
2006–2009   **BA (Hons) Ancient History (2:1), University of Nottsborough**
2004–2006   **A-Levels, Nottsborough School for Boys**
              English Language (A), History (B), Drama and Theatre Studies (B), AS Politics (B)
2001–2004   **GCSEs, Nottsborough School for Boys**
              2 A*s, 4 As, remainder Bs and Cs (10 in total)

OTHER SKILLS

- Proficient in Microsoft Word, Excel, Outlook and PowerPoint. Basic competency in Microsoft Access, Adobe Reader and Photoshop. Basic understanding of HTML and Web content management
- Typing speed of approx. 70 wpm
- Clean driving licence, four years

INTERESTS

Diving (PADI), triathlon (Nottsborough Team), tennis, 5th Dan tae kwon do coach

References available upon request

D.O.B: 16.10.1987
Nationality: British

CV EXAMPLE 2

Jocelyn R. Armstrong

The Vine, 18 Lois Drive, Peterborough, PE3 1GU, ENGLAND

tel: 09678 517435 (M), email: jocea13@ymail.com

A CONSULTING ASSOCIATE adept in winning and developing major accounts and relationships, and in managing very large international projects in strategy, customer service and operational review across a broad range of sectors.

OBJECTIVE: An MD/CEO/COO role in a service sector organisation with a particular interest in those involving NVO.

1987–date   **BYOO Inc.**
              T/o £1.5bn, a global operations, technology and review
              market leader

2006–date   **Rawlinson Pickett, Client Associate**
              Re-appointed to Client Associate with responsibility for
              greatly enlarged Group
              • Led Group strategy project, reporting to CEO, to assess
                market opportunities and development of options to
                increase Enterprise Value materially over 5 years
              • Played a central role in assessing attractiveness of options
                and developing the equity story with investment banks and
                the Board of Directors

              Strategy Practice Head
              Promoted to head the £10m+ UK transport strategy
              consulting practice
              • Appointed specifically to grow practice significantly over
                next two years

2002–05   **BYOO NVO Singapore, Managing Partner**
              Promoted to build a substantial NVO practice in Singapore

- Developed and gained adoption of strategy and market-entry plans for start-up of NVO business securing $10m seed-corn budget
- Created and owned whole business including hiring management team, developing operations blueprint and deal economics, selecting sites, negotiating contracts, implementing technology solutions, employee communications, client relationships, etc.
- Designed customer relationship management and shared services propositions for North American and UK transport, logistics, supply chain and wholesale clients
- Appointed as Managing Partner for Asia Pacific Operations, based in Singapore, directly responsible for P&L – £20m capex and £30m opex budgets – and 1,250 staff across region, serving clients primarily in the USA (Dow Jones 100) and UK (FTSE 100)

2000–02 **Unity Rail & Cargo, Client Associate**
Promoted to full equity partner and to build the relationship from scratch
- Led numerous assignments sponsored by the Group finance and strategy directors including peer group analysis and benchmarking, strategic value analysis and review of South American telco acquisition
- Oversaw an operational budget of *c.* £85m reporting directly to the IT director
- Scoped, estimated, organised and gave leadership to an IT department of *c.* 200 staff
- Managed a programme of approximately 80,000 man days of effort, with six distinct project streams, including finance, shared service, field force and knowledge management systems
- Planned the integration of two substantial IT departments following the acquisition of a major UK transmission company
- Grew consulting sales from zero to *c.* £20m

1999 **Office of BYOO, Global Managing Partner, NVO**

Appointed Programme Manager for head of $3bn global NVO practice

- Reviewed performance across the top-10 client contracts, supported client service reviews and developed programmes to roll out standard methods, tools and practices globally, resulting in the closure of two unprofitable arrangements

1997–99 **ES Water Company, Account Manager**

Promoted to Associate to repair the relationship with a major communications company

- Led all major projects with IT director's sponsorship including: geographic systems product selection, NVO programme management methods, field force product selection
- Co-led with customer operations director's sponsorship the team winning major contracts for field systems implementation and NVO
- Built revenue from zero in FY96 to £10m in FY99

Pre-1997 **FR Consulting across a range of sectors in CRM and Shared Services**

Invited to take a classic consulting career path leading from graduate to senior executive

- Led the team delivering the ITM strategy project for Rollo Stores Group, addressing customer segment profitability and customer experience across all channels
- Led the project for a pan-European customer service centre programme for JY Chemicals collapsing fourteen administrative centres into two contact centres
- Led a market entry strategy project defining the customer service capabilities that 'start-up' comms FM company, RTO, would take to market in Scandinavia
- Led a customer service strategy project defining the future operational vision of a major customer service function for RoRo
- Led a project defining the service strategy and business operations model for R2 across its varied customer base

- Acted as the subject matter expert in the FR-Spanish team developing an operations blueprint for the customer service function for Spanish electricity company, ESTL

QUALIFICATIONS　　James Wyatt College, Oxford University, IT, BA (First Class Honours)

LANGUAGES　　Fluent English, French and Spanish

PERSONAL　　Italian, married with two sons, willing to travel Hobbies include: classical music, opera, tennis and golf

CV TIPS

Here are some things to bear in mind:

Invest the Time
- Set aside a few hours when you aren't likely to be interrupted to think about and develop your CV.
- It's best not to develop your CV while you're at work; try and find some time at home at the weekend, when you are rested but alert.
- If you have objectives or personal review documents that have emerged from any scheduled review meetings over the past year (or as far back as five years if you can find them) with your manager, these can be useful aids/prompts to help clarify what to include on your CV.
- Focus on the benefits that you have brought to your organisation(s), in terms that people outside your company will understand.

- Refine your CV to emphasise those aspects you feel best illustrate your aptitude for a specific role or those sorts of role you are aspiring to, but I strongly recommend you do your tailoring after you have first developed the raw template as opposed to developing the whole CV with this in mind.

Keep it Confidential

Your CV is a confidential document containing information about you and where you live and work that you should seek to keep confidential. There is nothing to be gained by a general broadcast of the complete document. It should not be passed to anyone without your having first agreed with them:

- Why they need it
- What they will do with it
- Who else they might share it with
- What has to happen for you to have it removed from their records

Elements of your CV can be released in various media formats (LinkedIn, etc.) but never the CV in its entirety.

STEP 1: WRITE YOUR CV – KEY POINTS

- Don't hold back in selling yourself. You are the product here.
- Understand the pitfalls of hero worship and how setting realistic goals is much better for your peace of mind.
- Recognise that knowing who you are and projecting attitude, presence and substance is at least as important as your level of experience to the interviewer.
- Write your CV, based on the proven template.

STEP 2: REVEAL YOUR CAREER FRAME

If you hadn't gathered already, this book goes well beyond winning the job offer. Breezing through the interview only to discover that it is simply not the job for you is actually a far worse outcome than not being offered the role in the first place.

So in Step 2 we are going to reveal your *career frame*. It is a framework made up of:

- Predefined principles, or *values* as I prefer to call them
- A focus on achieving clear *goals*

In terms of the interview and your quest for career enhancement, your career frame will provide structure to your career-buying endeavour. After all, the interview is an opportunity to *buy* a career. So when you turn up to the interview you had better have your buying tools and rules with you. Your career frame helps you establish what you want from a job, so that you can progress rapidly towards your goals while ensuring that you stay true to your values.

DON'T WIN THE WRONG JOB!

Perhaps …

… if you had just asked for a little more clarity regarding the aspects that are important for you …

... if you had known going into the interview what those important aspects were ...

... if you had been more thorough in the interview process and given the interviewer a harder time ...

... you could have spotted the issues and withdrawn your candidacy gracefully or, better still, helped shape the opportunity into an ideal fit for you before agreeing to join the company. 'But for the power of hindsight,' you might say on finding yourself in this unhappy workplace, 'I could have avoided all of this pain and angst!'

We are going to prepare for and use the interview to ensure you never end up kicking yourself after the event because you have taken the wrong job.

TRIPLE-JUMP SYNDROME

There is a syndrome that I warn our candidates about called the 'Triple Jump', in which the candidate:

- **Hops** out of their cosy but less than ideal job into one that is not too far removed. Usually something simple has triggered the move, such as a colleague inviting them to an apparently greener pasture with reassurances that everything in the garden is rosy. Their diligence guard lowered by said reassurances, they ignore obvious warning signs. Having landed in their new role it transpires that the grass is not at all to their liking. They regret making the move, so they ...
- **Skip** a little further into a different company again before finally – you guessed it – reality dawns and they ...
- **Jump** into a role where they finally settle down.

How these triple-jumpers wish they had found the job they wanted in a single bound!

So imagine for the moment that you have indeed, unfortunately, just won the wrong job. The hindsight view from where you are would reveal clearly what you actually should have looked for in an ideal role in the first place. You can now *see* what you *need to see* to go for the right role.

In essence you will have absolute clarity about issues that fall under two headings – *values* and *goals*. But you needn't wait until you see these revealed in hindsight; we can draw them out in advance.

VALUES

Values are principles that are important to you. These might include such examples as:

- **Honesty/integrity**: I prefer to speak and hear the truth. Any compromise makes me uncomfortable; I feel compelled to make sure that the truth is outed.
- **Strong team ethic**: I like to feel part of a team who work and play hard. While I want to be recognised for my role and contribution I prefer to be rewarded for and to succeed at those things I cannot do alone.
- **Variety**: I can't do routine. I need to constantly change my surroundings and the challenges I face.

You need to drill into these just a little further to see why they are important. The majority of employees who feel out of sorts with their day jobs do so because one aspect or another of their role *conflicts* with their personal values.

If, for example, you value a great deal of variety in what you do and yet you find yourself repeating the same tasks at work over and over again, you probably become bored and ultimately you may decide that this reflects on the whole company, who do not seem to respect your strongly held value to vary what you do.

It is likely that if the company had understood your need for variety and been able to inject more into your role then your attitude and behaviours would have been more positive.

GOALS

There is so much written on the subject of goal setting and achievement (a lot of it overhyped rubbish in my view) that I want first to stress that this is not the focus of this book because your goals actually only play a bit part in the interview process on which we are focused here.

From an interview perspective it is your goals for the next two years that we need to nail. Specifically we need to reflect on:

- What you do to earn a living
- Who you do it with
- Where you do it geographically
- What terms you do it on
- What you achieve as you do it

How you want these areas to develop as you make a change will likely form your *professional goals*. It is a fact that if you land in a job that cannot provide you with the means to achieve a goal or goals that you consider imperative, then you are going to be disappointed.

VALUES + GOALS = CAREER FRAME

Your ideal job appointment is best described as being the one that takes you most rapidly to your goals while staying aligned with your values. In order to reveal your career frame you are going to complete an exercise called the 30-minute Burn. Let me reassure you that the output from this exercise has a direct bearing on the whole preparation process – all the way down to the questions you will ask in the interview itself. Every candidate I send out for an interview has completed this exercise – it is a simple yet powerful tool.

THE 30-MINUTE BURN

Set aside 30 minutes of your day when you know that you are not going to be disturbed. Have your watch or another timing device to hand. Settle down and get ready to learn something about yourself that you would ordinarily pay a coach a lot of money to extract.

The short time that this exercise takes is important for three reasons:

1. Because it only takes 30 minutes you are likely to actually do it.
2. You are unlikely to be able to spare the time to meditate for six months in a mountain retreat to enjoy a full discourse with your inner self.
3. The raw feelings are best left unpolished (for now).

So in the 30-minute Burn we spend:

- 10 minutes on values
- 10 minutes having a breather
- 10 minutes on goals

MY VALUES

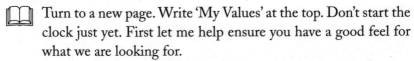 Turn to a new page. Write 'My Values' at the top. Don't start the clock just yet. First let me help ensure you have a good feel for what we are looking for.

In the 10 minutes you spend thinking about your values you are going to have a go at writing down all of the values you hold dear, in note form. You are going to do this by capturing the emotions you experience in both positive and negative situations.

You should be able to get a glimpse of your values when you are thinking about positive things, so during the exercise try visualising yourself in the following scenarios:

- With friends in a social setting
- With work colleagues or perhaps fellow students
- With teammates on a sports field
- With family and relatives
- Alone, just after you have achieved something that has made you feel proud of yourself

Consider what it is that makes you feel positive about these scenarios.

You will get a clearer look at the same values if you test them in a negative scenario, so now try visualising yourself:

- Falling out with a friend
- Finding out that one of your colleagues has let you down in some way
- Being left out of the team for a key game
- Having a disagreement with a family member
- Alone, following a crisis or calamity of some kind

Consider what it is that makes you feel negative about these scenarios.

By doing this you'll be closing in on the values in the middle.

Imagine for a moment that you are running your fingers across a piece of wood. When you travel with the grain it is smooth whereas if you go against it you feel the lumps. Similarly, on the one hand you feel positive when your values are supported and respected and on the other negative as you feel your circumstances going against the grain of your values.

The box below gives some suggestions as to how you might feel when situations go either with or against your value grain.

Positive outcomes with value grain	☺ YOUR VALUES ☹	Negative outcomes against value grain
Fulfilled		Lost
Happy		Sad
Content		Demotivated
Secure		Angry
Excited		Insecure
Motivated		Uncertain
Enthused		Bored
Confident		Unsure

We aren't looking for chapter and verse, just to capture the feeling. So in the burn you might scribble down:

*PEOPLE: Don't like being alone. Like lots of people around me who
I like and respect.*

You are either going with the value grain or against it – what is it?
What is the underlying value that makes you feel this way? Tease it
out. Write down the values that occur to you. Ten is plenty, any more
is probably overdoing it.

You can always come back and refine your list of values, but try to
use the pressure of the 10-minute time constraint to compile your list
as it will more likely get you honest results.

⏰ Give yourself 10 minutes on the clock and write down your
    values.

⏰ Stop the clock when you have written down 10 values or when
    the 10 minutes are up.

Now spend some time reviewing them. What would you say are your
top five? Which of your values do you feel most strongly about? Refine
them. So, if we take the example I gave above:

*PEOPLE: Don't like being alone. Like lots of people around me who
I like and respect.*

When you get the chance to reflect on this and refine it, this might
become:

*A SOCIAL ANIMAL: I need to be in the company of people, be they
new colleagues, friends or clients, as well as within easy reach of my
established circle. I like to work and play collaboratively.*

Well done. Take a 10-minute break. Leave the room. Have a stroll.

PROFESSIONAL GOALS

📖 Turn to a new page. Write 'My Goals' at the top.

You may well have written out lists of goals before and in all likelihood you have read or at least glanced through one or more of the many books on this much-covered subject. Despite any preconceived ideas you might have, please follow the guidelines below.

We are trying to answer the question: 'What are your goals for the next 24 months?' We take the 24-month period because it presses you beyond the one-year cliché. We usually overestimate what we can achieve in one year and we underestimate what we can accomplish in five. So two years is within touching distance yet it invites us to stretch our legs at the same time. Actually two years is an ample time frame in the contemporary career. Any shorter and your ability to make significant and meaningful strides is limited; any longer and you are into unknown, wider economic influences that are too hard to guess at.

Again, allow 10 minutes. You are simply writing down those things that occur to you as being worthy goals. If it's important to you and will enthuse you, then it is probably a worthy goal. Write the heading not the detail (you only have 10 minutes and you can elaborate later).

The SMART advice is sound when it comes to goals; make them:

Simple and clear
Measurable
Achievable
Realistic
Time constrained

Career goals naturally blend with much of your personal agenda:

- Where you live
- Your relationship and family plans
- What you do for relaxation
- How you keep fit and healthy

So, think about these factors during your 10 minutes, too.

🕐 Give yourself 10 minutes on the clock and write down your goals.

⏱ Stop the clock when you have written down 10 goals or when the 10 minutes are up.

Reread your goals. Go through and flesh out your notes, so that they are clear and precise. Check again that they meet the SMART criteria. So, a well-worded career goal might look like this:

HIGH PERFORMER: I will exceed my revenue and profit targets by better than 20% in each of the next two years and be recognised by winning a place in the 'High Performers Club' each year.

Or:

LAUNCH CONTROL: I will find and land an ideal first job by 31 March that:
1. *Leverages my degree (in a life sciences discipline).*
2. *Allows me to build a strong foundation (by challenging me to learn the business application of my science prowess).*
3. *Offers opportunity for rapid advancement (with both management and technical development loops if possible as I remain open as to which of these I take).*

Goals that sit between your career and your personal plans might read something like:

TRAVEL BUG: In the next twenty-four months I will travel to and have business meetings in at least five EU countries I haven't visited before as part of a new, more international, career outlook. In each country I will order a meal and engage in other basic courtesies in the local language.

Or:

FITNESS DRIVE: I will lose 15lb and improve my health by 15 June through a balanced regime of aerobic exercise (3 x per week), free-weight training (2 x per week) and rationing my drinking to no more than three days per week.

Now go back over your goals again and prioritise them, starting with the most important goal. The 30-minute Burn has provided you with the foundation material we needed to extract. You can now spend additional time reflecting on how best to tidy up the output.

CAREER FRAME = GOOD ATTITUDE

In the previous chapter I mentioned the importance of attitude as a key attribute that those who are seeking to fill positions are looking for these days (see pages 20–21). Candidates demonstrate good attitude more clearly and honestly when they are equipped with the personal insight that the career frame provides.

Just by capturing them you have taken an important step towards achieving your goals already. More importantly, by determining your values and goals you have provided yourself with clarity on your personal career framework. You now know what you want and need. My experience is that equipped with a well-structured CV and your career frame you sit in the upper 10 per cent of professionals who seek to better their careers simply because you are better self-appraised.

STEP 2: REVEAL YOUR CAREER FRAME – KEY POINTS

- Winning the wrong job is an avoidable disaster.
- Self-analysis in terms of your values and goals is the starting point.
- The triple-jumpers show us that the power of hindsight ultimately reveals the values and goals that are critical to us.
- Values + Goals = Career frame.
- Use the 30-minute Burn exercise to establish your career frame.

STEP 3: REVEAL YOUR CORE

You will recall that objective number one for any interview meeting is to answer the question:

'Do I want the job?'

Well, in order to answer this question you had better begin with a clear idea of the sort of job you are really looking for. Unless of course you fancy a run at the triple jump! (See page 34.) This is a good time to take a moment to assess what you are today, in your professional capacity, and what you want going forwards before you buy the wrong job.

So to complement the career frame (see pages 33–42), we are going to dig deeper into what you are and what makes you tick.

AT MY CORE I AM ...

This step begins with a question that my team and I ask of every candidate we provide career coaching to. Pretty much without exception our candidates respond with remarks such as:

- *'Hmmm, I haven't been asked that before. That's a good one.'*
- *'Oh! Bit stumped by that one. Good question. Give me a moment.'*
- *'Wow. You don't mess around do you? Tough one!'*

Here is the question exactly as we ask it:

'Imagine you are a stick of rock*: what does it say across the middle? What are you at your core?'

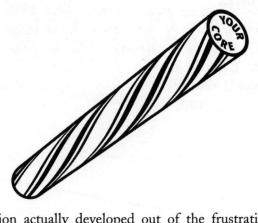

This question actually developed out of the frustration we felt at virtually all of the candidates we dealt with being somewhat deluded by their own professional self-image. They confused themselves and us by mistaking some of the labels they used internally within the organisation they worked for with what we were really asking them for. For example:

'I am general manager for an automotive parts company in Dubai with responsibility for direct sales, distribution and channel.'

This over-elaborates the point. 'Sales Manager' nails it!

So, we had brainstorming sessions, where we tried to come up with the right question. We tried a number of options over a period of years and finally found the question as it is written above to be the simplest and most powerful way to get to the answer that we needed.

---

* For anyone not familiar, a stick of rock is a type of hard, boiled-sugar confectionery in the form of a cylindrical peppermint-flavoured stick. The sticks often have a word or words throughout their length, so even when a bite is taken the text is still readable. Sticks of rock are traditionally sold at British seaside resorts with the name of the resort running through them.

The *core* description of what you are is helpful when it comes to considering a career step of any kind. When asked about the job that you do, the temptation is to come up with an elaborate explanation. However, keep reminding yourself that your answer should sit easily in the stick of rock. When you clear away all the clutter and distractions, this captures neatly what you do so that on entering the job market, from whatever standpoint, you can at least narrow your search to roles that come under this heading.

So answers to the stick of rock question should be simple and to the point:

- Salesperson
- Engineer
- Leader
- Entrepreneur
- Investor
- Inventor
- Cabinet-maker
- Craftsperson

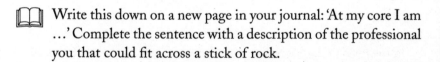 Write this down on a new page in your journal: 'At my core I am …' Complete the sentence with a description of the professional you that could fit across a stick of rock.

STEP 3: REVEAL YOUR CORE – KEY POINTS

- To answer the question 'Do I want the job?' requires first that you understand what sort of job you are really looking for.
- To understand what sort of job you are looking for you need to reveal your core.
- Answering the stick of rock question gets to your core.

STEP 4: PLOT YOUR CAREER TRAJECTORY

In this step we will develop your thinking beyond the career frame (see pages 33–42) to focus on the dream picture you might place in that frame. Your *dream career*.

To help you resist the temptation to buy the wrong career and instead hold out for the right option, we need to take stock of how you make important buying decisions.

HOW DO YOU BUY?

Job opportunities arise whether you are actively looking to move or you just happen to bump into an opportunity. Whatever the circumstances, you *buy* a new job:

- **Passive – not looking to move:** Jill had thought about a return to work following maternity leave but had yet to do anything about it. An acquaintance, Sally, mentioned she was setting up a nanny agency in the town. After a short conversation over a cup of tea they agreed to join forces. Jill *bought* Sally's business opportunity.
- **Active – looking to move:** Matt had been unhappy for ages with the lack of prospects in his job and had been scouring the job ads online for something that fired him up. He attended a few interviews but none of the roles turned out

to be any more inspiring than his current role. He spoke to some friends about his predicament and word got around that he was looking determinedly. Ashley picked up the phone to Matt as soon as he realised he had the job opening that he felt would fit. It did fit and Matt *bought* the move.

The interview you are preparing for actually represents a single stage in a *buying cycle*. If you are going to nail it then essentially we are going to have to ensure that you buy well.

You might not have thought about the interview as being part of a buying process, but you do indeed buy your career. It need not necessarily be sold to you, by which I mean that you might not feel the prospective employer is going out of their way to encourage you to join, indeed red carpets do tend to be reserved for rock stars. However, regardless of the selling that is going on on the employer's side, you do buy the role. It is your decision. You ultimately decide that the job is for you and once offered the role you accept the offer. You buy it!

PERSONAL BUYING DECISIONS

Each of us has a unique approach to buying. We take decisions about what we want every single day in our own particular way.

HOW DO YOU THINK YOU BUY?

What have you bought that requires care and forethought?

- Blu-ray player
- Computer
- House
- Car
- University/college
- Job?
- Career?

Professional buyers are trained to buy well. They are taught to see through their own particular nuances, to get beyond their emotions and ensure that they buy what they want and they buy it well. They don't fall foul of impulse buys or clever sales ploys. The rest of us are amateur buyers and are therefore likely to be inclined to more emotive reasoning. The way you make big buying decisions is personal to you. You do have an approach to decision making. Whether it is well refined or not doesn't matter. Your life experiences, the good decisions and the bad, have shaped your approach to buying.

It is important that you recognise your personal buying process in order that:

- You avoid some of the nastier outcomes that are possible when you allow your heart to rule your head.
- You ensure you extract everything from the interview that you will need to meet the tests you like to apply and going forward these will include a look at how well this opportunity sits in your career frame.

You can imagine how a lack of attention to their buying nuances commonly sees candidates emerge from their interview short of the information they need to make a critical buying decision – do I want this job?

You can't nail an interview unless you know what you need to answer this question. So have a go at the following exercise and let's see if we can get a handle on how it is that you buy.

OLD BUYING PROCESS

Start with a new page. Write the heading: My OLD Buying Process.

Take your time. Clear your head. Now think of one of the biggest purchases or key decisions you have had to make in your life, perhaps it was going to university or buying a house. Once you decide on the purchase/decision that you are going to use as the basis for this exercise, complete the phrase below in your journal:

1. When I made the decision to ...

Now rewind a little further and consider how you first decided that you needed this item or to take this course of action and try this one:

2. I had settled on the need for this because ...

This is a more challenging question as it explores how you chose from the many options available. Perhaps in this instance it was simply an impulse buy. For example, you walked in, bought the house and walked out. There isn't a right and a wrong here. If impulse buying is your way then you can just complete the first line of Point 3 below. However, it is more likely that you will have gone through several stages and the prompts below are designed to help tease these out of you. Take a little time and fill in the prompts that you feel help to capture the course of action you followed.

3. First I ...
   Then I ...
   I consulted with ...
   Also consulted with ...
   Checked that ...
   Allowed time for ...
   Rechecked by ...
   Finally ...
   Then ultimately ...

Now that time has passed and you have the luxury of hindsight, when you reflect on what went on as you made this big buying decision, how does it look to you as a process? Have a go at these final few prompts:

4. Do you feel this represents how you tend to make major decisions?
5. In hindsight was this a good call?
6. Is there anything you might do differently next time around?

You should find that, give or take a few stages and providing for refinements as you gain experience (we all evolve, all of the time), this is how you make buying decisions.

Now consider:

- How best to adapt this personal process of yours to the job-buying process you are entering into.
- What information will be required as a minimum to support your process?

NEW BUYING PROCESS

If you are at a stage in your career when you have made a job move or two, maybe more, then you have the added benefit of being able to make a comparison between the process you have captured here and the way you actually made the decision to accept jobs in the past. How close are they? Use this insight to tune the process – firstly as an account of what you actually did and secondly to develop what we are looking for here, which is a clearly defined, personal buying process you have used in the past. We can then take this process and enhance it to help ensure that you are better placed to buy the right job.

📖 New page. Write the heading: My NEW Buying Process.

You get to design your own buying process from scratch. It's up to you what goes in and what gets cut, but be sympathetic to what you have done before as this is how you bought naturally and for all of our flaws we are actually very capable of developing solutions that work quite well for our own particular preferences. So don't rip up your old buying process completely, rather enhance, improve and embellish it. If all you do is simplify the process by cutting an unnecessary step or two you will find that this will be a great help.

Knowing this personal process, recognising it as your approach, acknowledging its strengths and weaknesses and then adapting it specifically to the job-buying process will help you to avoid blind reliance on what we often describe as '… how I feel'.

*

Now that you have established how you buy, you are ready to look at how and why the interview is the ideal meeting:

- In which to explore *how* your dream is realised.
- To inspire people to *help* you realise your dream. I'll demonstrate for you how much more connected you will be to those people with whom you have been so honest and open.

Developing this clarity on where you want to get to needs to be done with half an eye on where you are now and where the momentum your career has acquired to date could take you. We call this *career trajectory*.

IT'S YOUR MISSION

The journey we take is dictated partly by aspiration, partly by capability and, of course, partly by factors that we can't control. Like it or not, you need time to develop your capability. Even those few born with extraordinary talent need to invest time to make the most of their skills.

- Can you be an experienced careerist without the benefit of time invested?
- Can your rocket vehicle fly faster regardless of experience?

You are going to have to answer these sorts of questions for yourself, but please take note of the warning I gave you against hero worship in Step 1 (see pages 14–15) and remember the quote:

'Don't measure yourself against other people, measure yourself against your own yardstick.'

CAREER TRAJECTORY

I'm sure you will have heard the old cliché about 'Shooting for the stars and hitting the moon'. Well, consider the common interview question:

'So what makes you think you are ready for this step up in your career at this time?'

Then reflect for a moment that your career does indeed follow a naturally phased trajectory of evolution, like a space mission.

EXPERT
55–Retirement: Your hard-earned experience prized by some. Your contact network will be critical to finding them. How rare is what you have to offer?

MATURE
40–55: You're cruising on your chosen path. Change is more difficult, but personal experiences make you increasingly valuable at what you do.

ROOKIE
30–40: You're applying all you've learnt. Inexperienced pilots are safer, more compliant and yet adept at change as the situation demands.

LAUNCH
30: Sees your career proper leave the launch pad.

PLANNING / TESTING
20–30: Early career grooves form. Variety here is key to allowing you flexibility later in your career.

FOUNDATION / EDUCATION
Through your late teens and into your twenties your degree or apprenticeship provides a firm foundation.

Building a truly great career is something you do in phases and with thoughtful planning. You can change direction and speed but you should always try to be clear and honest with yourself about which phase you are in and where the next milestone in your development lies before you move on.

If you overstretch too much you may get through the interview door and indeed hired into the seat, but it won't help you once you realise you have overstepped your true capability and experience.

That is not professional and it is *not* what this book is designed to help you achieve. Too often I have witnessed the over-promoted and overconfident trip up in an early charge for the line. The consequences aren't pretty.

KEY ADVICE

Don't tone down your ambition.

But

Do be very aware of the career phase you are in.
Do be honest and self-critical as you travel to your goal.

It is in blissful ignorance that we find the worst blunders. Those who don't bother to take the time to consider the career phase they are in; those who don't face or even acknowledge facts that are right in front of them. They will be confronted by facts either in a well-run interview or (far more grievously) after landing in a role that exposes their shortcomings.

CAREER TRAJECTORY TOOLS

Here are three tools that will help ensure that you nail down the following:

Question	Tool
Where are you on your career trajectory?	◎ Career bullseye
	⊞ Career benchmark
What does your dream career look like?	☁ Career vision/dream

When combined, the information you gather from using these three tools will give you a fairly accurate fix on where you are, a bearing on where you would like to head and a check that you have what you need to get there.

◎ CAREER BULLSEYE

Firstly we need to take a close look at what it is you actually do. The specifics of what you do, whom you do it for, who else competes in this marketplace and the broader characteristics of the sector within which the company operates are the important factors we need to clarify when we look at your career bullseye.

Your career bullseye is a precise definition of where you are today. It therefore changes as your career progresses. The career bullseye tool is not about setting goals, it's not about targets in that sense, it's used here as a measure of precision. It is the spot at the centre of your target today where:

- Your skills are in most demand.
- You might have a proven track record.
- You can probably prove the ability to deliver immediately (without the need for retraining).

The bullseye is distinct from the rings that ripple progressively further outwards because you might very well be able to do an okay job in a position that would fall into those outer rings, but clearly not with the same prowess.

Take, for example, a recently qualified graduate in geology (the science that deals with the physical structure and substance of the earth). I would expect their career bullseye to be:

- In a profession that requires geological prowess.
- In a company that has a proven graduate intake history for geologists.

Of course this graduate might choose a totally different career path. They might choose to place their foot on the first rung of a career in finance, for example. Such a step would be perfectly feasible but would almost certainly miss the bullseye and hit one of the outer rings (depending on how big the shift is). Taking this step means that:

- Their skills are less well aligned to the job, so they are not necessarily as well equipped as other candidates will be.
- They will likely need additional training, which will delay their ability to deliver in the role.

Both of these factors will negatively impact on a candidate's immediate value to an organisation and this will likely be reflected in the starting seniority and remuneration. So a step away from your bullseye represents career change and will almost certainly require you to accept some (or all if you go for an internship) of the risk that this entails for the organisation who are providing you with the training and development opportunity.

TARGETING YOUR BULLSEYE

If you are already some way further along your career trajectory with several years of experience behind you, then your bullseye is more easily picked out by reference to the immediate competitors to the company that you have the most experience with. These companies will pay you the most for your skills as on arrival you will most likely deliver immediate value.

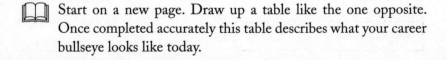 Start on a new page. Draw up a table like the one opposite. Once completed accurately this table describes what your career bullseye looks like today.

My career bullseye		
Bullseye definers (the key points that describe what you do, for whom and where):		
Organisations working in my bullseye	**Size (employees and revenue)**	**My thoughts on them**

If you are between jobs at the moment or just stepping on to the career ladder for the first time you have the luxury of being able to select a single organisation whom you like the look of or perhaps aspire to work for as the basis for this exercise. Then develop the bullseye table with their closely associated competitors.

If you are currently in a job, then those whom you know have competed for business with your current employer are likely to be the closest to the centre of the bullseye, as are those geographically closest to where you currently work. Put these down first. List those who do work in the same or similar sector but aren't necessarily head to head next. Then write down a sample of those who dabble while still presenting a threat.

The bullseye table is equally applicable regardless of the sector you work in. For example, museums, art galleries and charities all depend on and therefore compete for good people. In many cases companies in the not-for-profit sector are looking for willing, able and experienced volunteers, so you can imagine how competitive they are when it comes to attracting and retaining great people without whom they simply can't function. Whatever your bullseye definers are, there are organisations that prize your skills and experience.

See if you can get 10 companies on your list as a minimum, but ideally try to get more than 30 to provide a strong list of options that will help you to gain the clear view of your career bullseye that you need. The more there are, the more people are competing for your skills. Based on the simple laws of supply and demand, this means more upwards pressure on your value today. The more opportunities there are, the more likely you are to find interesting career pictures for your newly captured career frame.

Here's the table with a few sample entries, so that you can see the kind of information you should be including.

My career bullseye		
Bullseye definers (the key points that describe what you do, for whom and where): • Qualified nursery nurse • Full-time • Weekdays and weekends • Interim and flexible-term experience • Birmingham or commutable		
Organisations working in my bullseye	**Size (employees and revenue)**	**My thoughts on them**
XYZ Nurseries Ltd	450 / £14m (franchise chain)	I hear they work you hard but offer great benefits and holiday terms.
Clara's Nurseries Inc.	850+ / £31m	Have closed several nurseries after some bad reports. Not sure where they are headed. Birmingham has only been open for three years.
Get Active Gyms	11,450+ £536m	Crèche operation has won awards and I like the idea of being attached to a gym.

TARGETED RESEARCH

Have a go at selecting either your current company or one you are targeting within your bullseye and do some research on them. The kind of research that you can do depends on the type of company or organisation it is. You may be able to research online for news, reviews and announcements from the past 12 months. If you feel up to gaining a slightly more strategic view (not essential but certainly helpful) then search out the latest annual or interim report. Look out for indications on how the company is trending in terms of revenue and profit. What does the company's leadership say about the performance and where they are headed? How upbeat are they about prospects?

Organisations such as charities and those in the public sector depend on public funding, charitable donations, volunteer work forces and foundation trust funds to keep paying their way. The disclosure required of these organisations is usually at least as detailed (if not more so) as it is for those in the for-profit sector. Take a look at the numbers.

Even if the whole notion of understanding the mechanics of how business finances work is alien to you (and indeed terrifies you), I would encourage you to try to get as close as you can to the numbers and the funds that drive the organisation.

The answer to the question 'How does the organisation fund itself and remunerate its staff?' will provide you with a foundation as to where you sit in the organisation as a whole, and further, how best to negotiate your position and your progression within it. Knowledge is power could never be a more aptly applied cliché.

WANT A CAREER SHIFT?

I often hear very successful employees at all levels remarking that their dream lies in a completely dissociated employment arena. However, the further you move away from what you have experience in, the bigger the career shift. This lessens your ability to deliver from day one in your new job, which will affect your recognition and remuneration. Some people have genuinely reached the point where they can afford to ignore this and take a flight of fancy, but most need reminding that there is scope for satisfaction, fulfilment and indeed fun within their bullseye.

I find it helps to pose the question: 'What has to happen for you to develop your career within your current bullseye in a way that accelerates you to your career dream?'

This question could well be answered with a change in company to another in the bullseye that offers a role that steps in the direction of your career dream. Such a move plays to your strengths (as opposed to ignoring or running away from them) *and* develops your career positively.

⊞ CAREER BENCHMARK

To plot where you are on your career trajectory we need to do it with reference to something or someone else – you need a *career benchmark* to assess where you are today relative to your bullseye. We aren't looking for a detailed assessment, just a feel for what is happening around you now, inside the bullseye that you have just drawn up, by exploring what other people are doing, achieving and finding in it.

Questions such as 'How am I doing in my job?' or 'Where next with my career?' are benchmark questions because the answers have to be relative to something or someone else; i.e. they have to be benchmarked against a known measure.

For example, the statement 'I am a fast swimmer' is not as meaningful as 'I am the fastest swimmer over fifty metres in my county'. The speed of your swimming here has been given meaning by comparing it to others in your county.

RESEARCH

So to establish your career benchmark you need to pull together some of the key facts about your bullseye. Some research is required and you break this research into four areas:

1. Talk to people
2. Trade press, forums and events
3. Salary surveys
4. Reflection

I. TALK TO PEOPLE

The starting point for your research is to talk to people in your bullseye.

- Who within your current company or organisation can you have a confidential conversation with?
- Who do you know that works in the companies you have listed in your bullseye?
- Who do you know that works in a company just outside your bullseye?

- Who do you know who has previously worked either in or close to your bullseye?

And don't forget recruiters and headhunters who operate in or just outside of your bullseye. From first-jobbers to those in the twilight of their career, there are professionals who act as consultants and talent agents to employees of all descriptions and experience levels.

From the high-street agencies to headhunters just handling a few placements a year on to the boards of Fortune 500 companies, they are all helping connect the dots in this huge, chaotic puzzle. You are of value and interest to a professional recruiter somewhere, who will be happy to see how they might connect you to one of these dots and make a fee.

For employment agencies and recruitment consultancies you will find that since most of the leading firms advertise the vacancies they are seeking to fill online, you can simply enter your role and region (town or city) into a search engine and current vacancies will be listed. Look for the recruitment company that placed the advert. Similarly, the bigger jobs boards such as www.monster.co.uk and www.jobsite. co.uk present a simple route for you to get a list of the recruitment companies that operate in your employment area.

You can, if you want to, call these companies to talk about one of the live roles and develop the conversation from there.

For a guide to who the headhunters are it's worth tracking down a copy of *The Global Directory of Executive Recruitment Consultants* (www2.askgrapevine.com/publications/). This is not a cheap publication; however, any good business library will keep a copy so you can reference the printed version for the information that you need. You will quickly find all of the headhunters who specialise in your niche and in most cases the names and contact details of the actual consultants you should reach out to. Add these people to your list of people to talk to. Provided you are prepared to play in this small target market you should find a real friend once you find the headhunter(s) who owns your niche. Now would be a good time to plug them into your life. In exchange for the benefit of your insight (yes, you do have unique and valuable perspectives on the world as seen from your standpoint) and a free coffee or even lunch, they are quite happy to share what they know.

All of the various people that you talk to will see the state of play within the space from a different angle and perspective. The more people you talk to, the more information goes into your own personal (and fast-developing) insight into the whys and wherefores of opportunity within your career bullseye.

Start by having some conversations with colleagues who also work in your bullseye (ideally in a different company). Open the discussion by being clear that you are thinking about your own career from a planning perspective and would like to ask them some questions about the space in which they (and you?) operate. You want to pick their brains. Then ask them questions, such as:

- What is the top person in your team doing better than everyone else?
- Do you have a feel for what they are earning?
- Where in the team pecking order do you feel you fit at the moment and what are you doing to progress?
- What do you think are the opportunities for development over the next six months in this space?
- What do you think are the challenges/threats?
- Who is the company's standout star and where are they headed?
- How have successful people managed to move up in the business? How do they first get noticed?
- What development courses are people investing time in?
- Is there such a thing as a hero in your space who everyone aspires to emulate?
- If you could join one team/company at the moment, which would it be?

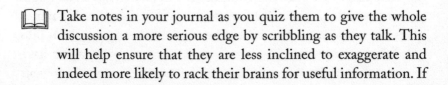 Take notes in your journal as you quiz them to give the whole discussion a more serious edge by scribbling as they talk. This will help ensure that they are less inclined to exaggerate and indeed more likely to rack their brains for useful information. If

you are talking with them on the phone, make sure they know you're making notes by asking them to slow down so that you can get an accurate record of what they're saying.

2. TRADE PRESS, FORUMS AND EVENTS

There are blogs, journals, clippings, newspapers and bulletins for every trade in every country in the world. A quick search will point you at forums where you can at least begin to find your preferred news medium, be it online or print. Aim for one that will help keep you abreast of your particular bullseye as well as what is happening in the wider sphere within which you operate.

When you get into a forum that looks and feels right to you, try and connect with other members. The challenges you face day to day and the queries you have will be more common than you might have imagined. If there is an open chat that everyone can see, put some general queries in there that will help you pick out those contributors who are most willing:

- Anyone have a feel for what we should pay as a day rate for a Unix engineer with eight years' experience based in New York?
- When is the next big trade get-together in the EU for our space?
- What does everyone read to keep abreast of crude oil price predictions these days?

Ask whatever you think will spawn some relevant responses. Don't try to be clever – just talk to people like you.

At trade fairs you can get a quick insight from and indeed do quick interviews with attendees who are there manning stands as well as delegates out on the floor. Your mission is part research and part self-promotion, but for certain you will, if you ask around, get pointed at the preferred trade column inches that are most useful. In among this noise are writ large the careers of those making stuff happen in your space. All of this material is more interesting when you consider the people behind it.

3. SALARY SURVEYS

How does your remuneration stack up to the sector? The most useful general salary surveys are published within trade forums and are typically available in recent versions for free on the Web. Have a go at entering a search along the following lines into your preferred search engine:

Country+Role+Salary survey

Good business libraries usually carry detailed salary surveys for virtually all trades and in a library you get the benefit of free help to dig out the particular data you are looking for.

While often an abused measure, earnings are a helpful benchmark because they are a very measurable and comparable aspect. What you are earning relative to those doing similar roles should become of real interest to you, particularly as your career matures.

In a fair world there ought to be a link between the shareholder value you deliver and the remuneration that you receive:

A self-employed window cleaner owns 100 per cent of the stock in their own business. If they do one more window they will personally be directly remunerated for the additional value brought into the business. If they hire another cleaner, they will need to decide what to pay them and then calculate how much work they will both need to do in order to justify all costs and leave some profit over for investment in, for example, the new van they are going to need next year.

Such commercial essentials remain the same whether you work in a museum, a publishing house, a bank, a hotel or indeed any line of business. Someone has to count and allocate the pennies.

As the organisations we are employed by become ever larger and more complex, we can become so disconnected from the business owner that we are inclined to forget or ignore these principles and I find it helpful to remind candidates of this key connection. Ultimately we are rewarded for the work that we do on behalf of a company owner by that company owner.

This perspective captures the whole premise for employment. The better your grasp of this fundamental point and the more in tune with it you are, the more likely you are to be able to develop your career in a way that meets your values and goals, but that also provides you with the remuneration you richly deserve.

So whether or not money is one of your main motivations, don't lose sight of how important it is to the owner of the business and to the success of the enterprise as a whole.

4. REFLECTION

While you can describe clearly where you are in terms of your own workplace and the immediate management structure within which you sit, it is trickier to answer the following:

- Where will your career lead if you do nothing?
- What do you want your career to become?
- What could your career become? What are the possibilities?

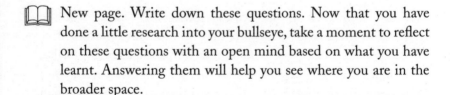 New page. Write down these questions. Now that you have done a little research into your bullseye, take a moment to reflect on these questions with an open mind based on what you have learnt. Answering them will help you see where you are in the broader space.

Hopefully you will see clearly where the opportunities lie. You will begin to see yourself relative to these opportunities and appreciate what you have to do to seize them.

However sketchy it might be at the moment, what you have captured here serves as a benchmark for where you are today relative to your bullseye. Revisit your benchmark periodically and reassess it. The world doesn't stand still and neither does your bullseye.

💭 CAREER VISION/DREAM

Where are you headed? Where do you want your career trajectory to take you? These questions invite you to do a little daydreaming.

Imagine for a moment that there might be such a thing as a utopian role out there for you, one that fulfils you, inspires you and allows you the ideal balance in your life. What ingredients do you think such a role would include?

📖 Turn to a new page. Write the heading: Dream Job Ingredients.

I went back over forms completed by some of our past candidates to dig these examples out for you to help get your ideas flowing. I have preceded the candidates' ingredient descriptions with the one word that I think best captures what they have written. You might find it helpful to use this style also:

- **Creative**: Roaming brief to assess creativity and bring it to bear across company.
- **Downshift**: Three-day week.
- **Title**: Chief Marketing Officer.
- **Flexi**: Work from where I like and when I like.
- **Interest**: Significant shareholding in business.
- **Reward**: A company van I can use on my time.
- **Travel**: Every week to a new country in EU.
- **Variety**: I don't want to have a clue what I am doing each day until after breakfast!
- **Independence**: Left entirely to my own devices and delivering to quarterly metrics.

So, what's your dream? Have a go at brainstorming this. There are no wrong answers and you should not dismiss anything that comes to mind. It might help you to think of someone you know or who is well known that you feel has the sort of role you would like to have. This exercise should be fun, so make sure you don't press yourself to complete it if you are finding it difficult or hard work.

Take the exercise one stage further by highlighting those ingredients that you would place most importance on if you wanted to make sure you realised them within two years.

Now use the highlighted notes to prioritise your top five. By doing this you will really start to pin down some of the ingredients that are

most important to you. This is a taste of your *career vision*. Take a look
back over your journal notes. Now you have your:

◎ Career bullseye	A list of the companies with the same or similar focus to your current organisation. Minimum 10 but ideally over 30.
▦ Career benchmark	How you are doing relative to the space and how you feel your company/organisation shapes up.
◌ Career vision/dream	Top five ingredients for your utopian role.

You now know where you are on your career trajectory because these
elements combined allow you to fix your current position and you
should also see the direction your momentum will take you in. You
have the information you need to make wise decisions about your
career steps from here.

STEP 4: PLOT YOUR CAREER TRAJECTORY – KEY POINTS

- The interview is part of a buying cycle for a new job.
- How do you buy? You need to reflect on your personal approach to making big decisions as you move towards the key career purchase that an interview is designed to yield.
- Clarity on where you want to get to needs to be viewed with half an eye on where you are now and where your natural career momentum takes you.
- Use three tools to plot where you are and where your career is heading:
  - Career bullseye
  - Career benchmark
  - Career vision/dream
- Combining the results from the exercises completed using these tools will fix where you are on your career trajectory.

STEP 5: CAPTURE YOUR USPs

'Why would I hire you?'
'Well?'
'I'm waiting …'

Did you think the interviewer was going to let you gloss over this small point? Believe it or not, most candidates really do allow themselves to trip up on questions as obvious as this. The first sign that they are struggling is:

The pause. 'Did they really just ask me that question? I thought this was going well and that they liked me!'

Then the stare and often the pupils dilate. 'They really did ask me that!'

Followed by the blink and the look away. 'Buy time.' ('Maybe throw in a cough to clear my throat, too.')

Inside they scream: 'Okay, okay, I have to sell myself really bluntly here. Don't overdo it though.'

I have learnt through experience that candidates at all levels and phases of their career have a strong tendency to be quite shy and reserved about selling themselves. So we have to be quite brutal. This is not a time to hide your light under a bushel. The interview is an invitation to take centre stage and describe you as a professional, taking particular care to emphasise those features and achievements that will most appeal to the interviewer. In short, a question such as 'Why would I hire you?' is the invitation you have been waiting for – *to sell yourself.*

HOW TO SELL YOURSELF

Selling yourself is not something you do every day. You might sell your ideas to your colleagues, lecturer, parents, workmates or superiors, but it isn't you on the shelf. So how do you go about doing this?

Well, you need to be equipped for all eventualities. Interviews come in many shapes and sizes. So in order to ensure that you nail that interview you need to be prepared and to practise selling yourself.

Let's begin with what you actually want to communicate. What is it about you that makes you an attractive candidate to the interviewer? How would you answer the question I just posed? 'Why would I hire you?'

The answer to this ought to emerge from your unique selling points. Your USPs. These are the differentiators you should be rightly proud of and which, all other things being equal, the interviewer ought to find highly compelling. You do not want to leave an interview meeting and realise that you didn't get these points across in a clear and memorable way.

In order to help you draw out your USPs, here are two exercises that we often do with our candidates.

YOUR ELEVATOR PITCH

The elevator pitch is the one you have in readiness for the surprise interview where, for example, you bump into the CEO in the elevator and she says, 'Hi, I'm Rosalind the CEO. Who are you and what do you do for us?' With just 15 seconds or so to ride to the fifth floor you need to have an elevator pitch that you can deliver with confidence.

Developing your own elevator pitch is the simplest and quickest way to get to your most important USPs. The following example gives you an idea of the sort of response that would work well.

I'm Jane McFadden. I joined as an intern six months ago with a top diploma in marketing. I'm pleased to say that out of eight interns I have been selected for permanent appointment in the marketing team where I'm now helping research the EU client base. My natural flair is to sniff out exploitable opportunities that lie embedded in the big data stock we have accumulated – it's more art than science – I love it! I try to gain as much insight as I can into the business from the top down so I try to spend as much time as I can with the CMO and the marketing director.

So you can see that the elevator pitch is a punchy overview that gives prominence to your USPs. If the interviewer (used in the loosest sense of the word here as this is an impromptu meeting) leaves the session and recalls your USPs then the pitch has been effective.

    Have a go at your elevator pitch. Imagine you are in that lift with your boss's, boss's, boss's boss. They have asked you the question: 'Who are you and what do you do for us?' You take a breath and …

What would you really like to deliver here? This is an interview. A fairly bizarre one, but ultimately all interviews are weird meetings. Don't look for perfection on the first draft – you won't find it. Rather aim simply to get something down and then play with it.

YOUR FAB

Features, Achievements and Benefits = FAB

The FAB provides you with crucial insight as you prepare for an interview because it sets out all of the important information that you must weld into the interviewer's mind during the interview itself. Candidates often struggle to get going with this exercise, but once they do they find it very helpful and insightful.

So, what is a feature, an achievement and a benefit?

If you ran your own small watch-repair business in your spare time while still at school, then that is a *feature*.

If the business thrived and you ended up hiring four staff to work for you before then selling the business for £10,000 by the time you were 20 years of age, that is an outstanding *achievement*.

The *benefit* of this would then best be described in a tailored way for the specific audience. It might look something like: 'I'm a self-motivated entrepreneur who looks for and capitalises on gaps in the market where clients would really appreciate and buy a quality solution.'

Draw up a table with three columns. Write the column headings 'Features', 'Achievements' and 'Benefits'. Now have a go at getting down some of your features first. Ignore the achievements and benefits for now. Just write a list of the features that you think deserve a mention. You can prioritise and edit later. If you have used Facebook extensively review it to remind yourself of what you have done. This history can help you realise that you do indeed have some features to shout about. Aim to write down at least five features. Ideally you will come up with a lot more; in which case go back over the list and pick out your top five. Here are a few example features:

- Club captain at school
- Father of four children
- Ran two marathons for charity
- Commuted to Spain for three years
- Exceeded target in financial downturn of 2009
- Led a team of 15 to a record quarter
- Developed a property in Florida
- Played hockey for college
- Keen golfer (16 handicap)

Once you have got your list of key features, then fill in the achievements and benefits to draw out the FAB. See the example table opposite. It shows a FAB for three different people. What it shows you is that from painter–decorator, to graduate, to entrepreneur, this exercise applies equally across the whole spectrum of professional life.

Features	Achievements	Benefits
Set up a small watch-repair business part-time out of school at 15 years of age.	Aged 20 had staff of three technicians and one administrator. Due to other commitments and a healthy offer I sold the business for £10,000.	Self-motivated entrepreneur who looks for and capitalises on gaps in the market where clients would really appreciate and buy a quality solution.
MSc Engineering with Honours.	Won the year prize for dissertation on 'Creativity in Design Thinking'.	A naturally creative thinker who also self-analyses methods and helps others to help me, thereby imbuing teams with enhanced creativity.
Eight years apprenticed to leading regional painter–decorator.	Owner unequivocal in that he found me to be the most proficient and able special-effects painter he had ever worked with!	Able to turn client vision into reality in painted design finishes that truly differentiate and result in commendation, recommendation and new custom.

Your FAB is the heart of your personal sales message. These are the attributes that point to your being able to deliver a good service to your next employer. We will be selecting extracts from here to use in the interview process.

With your FAB completed you should go back to your elevator pitch and look at it again. Does the pitch efficiently and powerfully sell you? Is the content sufficiently clear about the achievements and benefits that present your key features in the best light?

Have another go at a draft that you can commit to memory. You don't know when your next interview will be. It could be in the elevator tomorrow afternoon with someone who you are destined to spend the next 10 years working with.

If you make sure that your FAB is communicated at an interview you will nail it as your capability to do the job will be a given. It is your attitude that they will buy and communicating your FAB to them will ensure they get a positive feel for yours.

HAVING A LAUGH

Stand-up comedians usually find that their best source of material is themselves; their own peculiarities, habits and nuances. It is good for us all to laugh at ourselves as it is both healthy and instructive.

Comedians who are just starting out use the FAB technique. They look at the *features* that define who they are, their *achievements* (or lack of them) and then consider the funny side (the *benefits* or punchline). You too might find it helpful to smile or even laugh at yourself in a healthy way as you look at yourself through this lens. By not taking yourself too seriously you get closer to the real you.

STEP 5: CAPTURE YOUR USPS – KEY POINTS

- We started with the question: 'Why would I hire you?'
- Capturing your USPs enables you to answer this question.
- In order to capture your USPs use two exercises:
  - Elevator Pitch – this is the simplest and quickest way to get to your most important USPs.
  - FAB – dig deeper still to seek out the features, achievements and benefits that really define you.

STEP 6: DRAFT YOUR STORIES

You will use stories to communicate your achievements, specifically those achievements that categorically point to your ability to deliver what the interviewer needs. These stories are really helpful when it comes to some of the more challenging questions you might be asked. We'll look at how and where to use them in more detail in Step 8; for now you're just going to draft your stories.

CASE STUDY

Take the true story of the forklift-truck operator in a warehouse in Sheffield, England.

On the surface of it, Pete was pretty much your average forklift-truck operator, albeit a young one. He lived within a mile or so of his workplace, with a wife and a young daughter. He had been with PRP Logistics Ltd for just over 18 months. But Pete wasn't just any forklift-truck driver.

Pete had only been with PRP a few months when he became somewhat bored with the mundane routine. To entertain himself he started thinking about the efficiency of what he was doing each day on his truck.

Pete figured out that he could halve the average time it took to load a truck. He shared his thoughts with his boss who was quick to point out all the reasons why it wouldn't work. He stressed how bringing the goods required for a given truck to a holding bay near to the loading ledge before the truck even pulled up would contravene health and safety guidelines.

Pete didn't give up. He was sure that the entrenched procedures he was working within were hugely inefficient and he was becoming obsessed with proving that he was right.

Eventually the regional head heard about Pete. It so happened that the region was under pressure to improve space utilisation by a significant amount and were also having their spending budget cut. The regional head asked to see him.

At first Pete's ideas were tried out in only small ways. But as they proved to be very effective he was invited to help re-engineer more and more of the logistics processes on the warehouse floor. From his forklift driver's seat Pete got to figure out new procedures, test them, prove them and then they would be rolled out across the group.

Just as he was really starting to get into all of this and find real satisfaction (and fun!) in what he was doing day to day for a living, a new company moved into the area and set up in a large refurbished facility nearby. Several of Pete's colleagues had been invited for interview by the company, who were setting out to aggressively poach PRP's people and so were offering significantly more money and improved flexibility. Pete was persuaded to go along for an interview himself.

Now you might have some inkling of where this is headed. Think about Pete's situation for a moment and ask yourself the following questions:

- How should Pete apply?
- How do you think he should weave his story into the interview?
- What are the three or four points that Pete should ensure the interviewer recalls about him as he leaves the meeting?

TELL YOUR STORIES

The purpose of these stories is to highlight achievements in your career to date that best illustrate that you can deliver all that the job you are interviewing for requires. Look back over your journal at your career frame (see pages 33–42), your stick of rock core (see pages 43–45) and your USPs. Now look over your FAB carefully (see pages 71–74). These will help you find examples from your recent career experience that can be used to promote you, the professional, and specifically demonstrate how your achievements were accomplished.

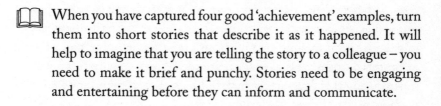 When you have captured four good 'achievement' examples, turn them into short stories that describe it as it happened. It will help to imagine that you are telling the story to a colleague – you need to make it brief and punchy. Stories need to be engaging and entertaining before they can inform and communicate.

Set the scene with a grabber (a headline that grabs the interest because it hints at the interesting story to come) if you wish:

- 'That reminds me of one of the hardest lessons I have had …'
- 'There was a very nasty situation in our Northern office that could have caused a meltdown …'

Here are two example stories to give you an idea of how to write your own:

EXAMPLE I: EARLY RETAIL

In the summer holidays for three consecutive seasons I worked for the clothes retailer Fat Face, helping to promote their new lines at student fairs and at major gatherings such as festivals. It was hard work but I loved it. To do it well you really had to focus on the people you met and quickly jump into their lives, their lifestyles and their fashion preferences. I think I learnt the real meaning of empathy from those three summers.

We were individually scored and given bonuses for sales we made. Each year I worked my way up the leader board so that by year three I was top for the Southern region.

My retailing backbone comes from living among the clients. I know how and why this group of people buy clothes so I can help them feel great about it. I know I'm doing them a favour because I know I'm helping them feel and look great!

EXAMPLE 2: HOTEL/LEISURE

I sometimes pinch myself – I feel so fortunate. I had worked in two roles within hotels during my first three years: first as a waitress and then as head of the reception desk. When the sommelier resigned I was sad as we had become good friends and he had got me interested in the vast world of the vintner from grape to glass. He had to work out three months' notice and I persuaded him to really show me the ropes during this time before he left. I have never been able to get over the enthusiasm he instilled in me. It continues to grow to this day.

To be able to combine my hobby with my job makes me feel very lucky.

That customers seek and respect my opinion and then thank me when I get recommendations spot on still thrills me.

Can you see how these stories draw on the features, achievements and benefits I showed you how to draw out in Step 5? By combining the entertaining communication tool of the story with the powerful FAB you are preparing to deliver the essential messages you need to convey in an interview. But more importantly you are going to deliver them in a way that will be remembered.

PROMPT SHEET #1

Type up your four stories, as you will take them into the interview with you to help prompt your responses and delivery during the meeting. This is *Prompt Sheet #1* (see page 146).

'CHALK AND TALK'

If it helps you to describe your story clearly in an interview you might consider using simple diagrams that you can hand-draw either on a small board or a sheet of paper. We call this 'chalk and talk' and it's particularly useful for illustrating structure, numbers and technical concepts. If you like this idea then you must simplify, refine and then practise your drawing(s).

Your illustration should take no longer than 30 seconds to draw and you should be able to talk as you draw.

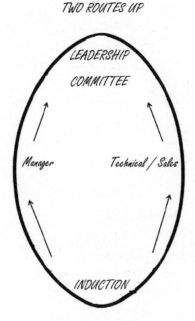

The impact of the delivery is far higher if you ask: 'Do you mind if I draw this? It will help to illustrate how I came to understand this one.' Take out your board or sheet of paper then reproduce the simple drawing that you have been practising. Another benefit of producing a drawing is that it is something you can leave behind as a reminder!

STEP 6: DRAFT YOUR STORIES – KEY POINTS

- Look back in your journal for your USPs and your FAB.
- Capture your most relevant achievements as short, entertaining stories and type them up.
- This is Prompt Sheet #1 that you will take into the interview with you to help prompt your responses and delivery during the meeting.

STEP 7: RESEARCH THE ROLE

Elevator pitches and chance encounters aside, the interview will almost certainly be a planned and scheduled affair. The pre-appointed time, place and style of the meeting will be agreed well in advance. It is possible that you might know the interviewer or that you know someone who does. Equally you might know quite a lot about the company and indeed have encountered them within your space many times.

Using the time you have prior to the meeting to learn as much as you can about the role, the interviewer and the company is imperative.

More information now = **Less** needed at interview = More **time**

Quite simply the *more* information you know in advance, the *less* information you have to discover on the day, allowing you precious *time* to take the discussion further and faster while you concentrate on positively influencing proceedings.

When beginning any research exercise it helps if you are first clear about the question you need answered once all of your findings are gathered in. This clarity will help drive the research process and will give the findings meaningful context.

There are two key questions you need to know the answers to. You need a good understanding of the job you are being considered for – *What is the role?* – and how the company is going about selecting their preferred candidate – *What is the selection process?* These are pretty broad and far-reaching questions because each scratch of the surface reveals so much new information.

In this step I am going to share with you the framework that I use to help ensure I have a good handle on any search assignments I accept. You should find this helps you to cut to the essentials and answer the two key questions.

I KNOW NOTHING

If you really want to know the facts, first begin with a blank page.

The clearing out of all the clutter and preconceived notions is a good first step to any well-founded research exercise. The bits and pieces of information you have gathered up over time are likely to be outdated at best and at worst complete fabrications that began small but grew with the telling.

Too often we encounter great people who have had their attitudes poisoned towards one employer or another in their bullseye by the remarks of just one of their colleagues. A sample size of one is insufficient; their experiences are barely relevant to your research. You will have to be really rigorous to make the research findings meaningful.

When you accept you know nothing you have everything to learn from scratch. You will be more likely to be critical and suspicious of unofficial sources and data that has not been audited.

Your determination to check and verify all of your information with several sources will help ensure accuracy and currency.

WHAT IS THE ROLE?

Some roles are more easily specified than others. For instance, an odd-job person is required or expected to do odd jobs and as the name suggests these are not predefined. At the other end of the spectrum, non-executive roles are notoriously tricky to pin down in a written specification.

JOB SPECIFICATION

Do you have a job specification or at least a brief description of the role? Behind any job advertisement or identified role there will be a more detailed specification. You can ask for this additional information, particularly where there is a recruiter involved, but internal human resources people can usually help. Be sensitive to the fact that many roles will be treated as confidential until you have reached the point of being an acknowledged candidate for the post, so there is often a catch-22 situation in which you don't know the detail of the role sufficiently well to know if you want to apply to become an acknowledged candidate, which is a prerequisite of getting more detail to enable you to decide. Frustrating I know.

Before a headhunter begins a search they invest a significant amount of time ensuring that they understand precisely what the client is looking for. One of the big traps we can fall into is thinking we know what is required only to find out our shortlist is somewhat wide of a mark that could have been better understood at the briefing stage.

We are very suspicious of job specifications issued by human resources departments. These tend to be boilerplate samples that have been completed more in the interests of ticking boxes to gain internal approval for the hire than to describe what is really required.

What follows is the questionnaire that headhunters use to specify a role with a client.

SEARCH ORDER

Contact Details

Job order no._____   Date: ___/___/___   Consultant: _____

Client:_____

Address:_____

Tel no:_____   url:_____

Contact: _____   Position: _____

email:_____

Qualifying Questions

Why is the position open? _____

How long has the position been open for? _____

Have you looked internally? _____

Have you advertised? _____

[1]*What other sources are you using?* _____

Have there been any offers to date? _____

Have there been any turndowns to date? _____ Why? _____

Are there any candidates still in contention? _____

What is your degree of urgency for this position? _____

Is this a newly created position? _____

[2]*What is your ideal start date?* _____

Job Description

[3]*What are the main duties and responsibilities?* _____

_____

[4]*Title?* _____ Reporting to? _____

Describe an average working week: _____

_____

Will there be travel involved? _____

How many staff supervised? _____

What is the background of the ideal candidate? _____

[5]*Where would he/she be working now? (i.e. competitors)* _____

Any particular organisations in mind? _____

[6]*Any specific individuals?* _____

What qualifications are preferred? (education and professional qualifications)

_____

Do you have a preferred age range? _____

Describe your management style: _____

How would you describe the culture of the company? _____

[7]*What sort of personality do you require?* _____

When all is said and done what is the most important quality the person you are looking for should have? _____

[8]*Assume you have hired a great candidate for this and we have jumped forwards 12 months from today – they have done fantastically well – what 3 things impress you most about them?*

1._____

2._____

3._____

Compensation

[9]*What is the salary range of the position?* Low: £ _____ Mid: £ ____ High: £____

If an outstanding candidate is currently at or near the top of the range can, *not will*, you go higher?

If yes, by how much? _____

[10]*Bonus?* _____ How calculated? _____

Company performance? _____ Personal performance? _____

Guarantee? _____ Car? _____ When is first review? _____

How much can it be worth? _____ Scheduled reviews? _____

Commission? _____ Profit sharing? _____ O.T.E? _____

Are there any fringe benefits associated with this package? _____

Life assurance? _____ Medical insurance? _____ Relocation package? _____

Pension?_____Others?_____

Opportunity

(If old position) What happened to the last person in this position? _____

What are the long-term prospects for a first-class candidate? _____

What is special or unique about your company/opportunity compared to your competitors? _____

How would you describe your company's image? _____

How many years have you been in business? _____

What is your annual turnover? _____ No. of employees? _____

What is the growth record over the last 5 years? _____

Do you have any expansion plans? _____

Who are your major competitors? _____

Do you have a corporate brochure? _____

[11]*Why would exceptional talent join you at this time?* _____

_____

Interview Information

To whom will this position report? _____

What is his/her background? _____

_____

[12] *What is the interview process? (How many – with whom – testing?)* _____

_____

When you interview, what kind of questions do you ask? _____

What is your company's dress code? _____

You don't need to grasp all of this before you arrive for the interview but consider each question and imagine how helpful it would be to have that information ahead of sitting down opposite your interviewer. The more insight you can get – particularly into the key questions (those numbered and highlighted in italics on the form) – prior to the interview the better.

THE KEY QUESTIONS

1. **What other sources are you using?** Getting a feel for the approach being taken to fill a vacancy will give you an insight into the importance and urgency of the position. From 'We are just having a general look and if we find someone great!' to 'We have got every available resource on this, it is a critical fill right now!' and everything in between. Clarifying this point also enables you to gauge what other candidates will be on their radar.
2. **What is your ideal start date?** It is helpful to check that the company's timing matches yours at an early stage.
3. **What are the main duties and responsibilities?** This and the following five questions all aim to tease out more than would be included as part of a standard role specification. These are the factors that will really help you decide if the job is for you. Obviously the main duties and responsibilities will be touched on

in the specification but try to understand what is really required of the role.

4. **Title?** There are often two aspects to this – title and designation. The title supposedly captures what you do while designation (if you have one) specifies the grade you are on for internal seniority purposes; for example – Regional Treasurer (Grade: Assistant Manager). It is worth getting a feel for both and, furthermore, comparing yourself where you are able with others whom you know in the hierarchy to see if you are well aligned. Is this a step up, down or sideways?

5. **Where would he/she be working now? (i.e. competitors)** This helps you to clarify how they view the market and what their preconceptions about you and your background might be going into the process. If they prize individuals from the big gorilla in the market (the biggest company among its peers) then the fact that you are from one of the smallest will need to be tackled by you in your positioning for the role.

6. **Any specific individuals?** This is extremely helpful to know in so far as it enables you to see who you are likely to be measured against.

7. **What sort of personality do you require?** I have touched on the importance of attitude but this means different things to every hiring authority, so if you can lift the lid by asking how they would describe the personality of the ideal individual, again you are gaining useful insight.

8. **Assume you have hired a great candidate for this and we have jumped forwards 12 months from today – they have done fantastically well – what 3 things impress you most about them?** If there was just one question out of those listed here that you could know the answer to, it would be this one. What this question does is to ask Question 3 again, but in a more meaningful way. By going forwards in time and looking back at a job well done we are helping the employer to reflect on what is really important.

9. **What is the salary range of the position?** You might as well know the answer to this early on as it won't change much, if at all, later and you are investing time here so make sure that you aren't going to win a role that you simply can't afford to accept.

10. **Bonus?** Whatever the role there may be scope for recognising good contribution with a bonus reward, whether cash or otherwise. How does it work?

11. **Why would exceptional talent join you at this time?** It is worth visiting this before the interview and in more depth at the interview. Get as much of a feel as you can as to what the organisation does to deserve the loyalty of its people and what it is doing that means they deserve more. How do they sell themselves?

12. **What is the interview process? (How many – with whom – testing?)** Clarity on this at the outset helps settle your own expectations. Bear in mind that in almost all cases the employer does what most of us do when we estimate any piece of work – we tend to underestimate it. So there will usually be at least one more stage than they suggest and it will take 25 per cent longer to complete.

Getting some of this information may not be straightforward. Consider the following tactics:

- Call HR: 'Hello, I am due in for an interview next Tuesday and I had a few questions around the process. Please can I ask …'
- Call a friend who works there.
- Call a friend who used to work there.
- InMail someone you are connected to on LinkedIn who works there/used to work there.
- If you are going through a recruiter or agency then pick their brains. If they don't know the answers ask them to find out for you.

All of this digging will yield rich rewards in terms of clarifying the focus and framework for the meeting and the process you are going into. This will help steer your preparation with a great deal more precision than any amount of guesswork.

WHAT IS THE SELECTION PROCESS?

Interviewers are, for the most part, ordinary people who have been thrown an extraordinary ball: 'Go ahead and choose your team.'

So let's have some empathy with the interviewer. Our priority, of course, is looking at the interview from your (the candidate's) perspective. But we should take a moment to look at the task of hiring people from the point of view of those who actually have to make hiring decisions.

- What are they looking for? (How do they decide this?)
- How do they find them? (How do they know they have found them?)
- How do they recruit them into the business? (How do they ensure they land those selected?)

BECOME THE INTERVIEWER FOR 15 MINUTES

Put yourself in the interviewer's chair. Look at the candidate sat opposite (in the mirror) and ask yourself: 'Do I want to hire this individual?' As you consider the person in the mirror try to be neither overly critical (a very common problem) nor zealously overconfident (less common but just as serious a flaw). Rather take a neutral view of yourself. Then begin to objectively assess yourself as a good interviewer would. Have both the role specification and your CV to hand.

Glance at one important aspect of the job specification, then to the mirror and then the CV. See yourself being hired for the role but acknowledge straight away any and all of the hurdles the hiring authority will have to clear to make that decision to hire you. Look at another aspect of the job spec, and so on. This exercise can be completed in just 15 minutes or so and I guarantee you won't be far off the mark in terms of how the actual process will unfold. If anything, the real interviewer will be far easier on you than you were on the mirror!

Putting yourself in the interviewer's chair will help you to reflect on what sort of people typically sit there. I think I can confidently assure you that the majority of interviewers you will meet will likely have a few traits in common:

- They will be poorly prepared for the interview.
- They will rely primarily on intuition and feeling to guide their decision making.
- They will take few notes and may well alter their views as to how they feel about you on reflection after the meeting.

But since we are setting out to nail that interview it would make more sense not to give yourself an easy ride. It is safer to assume that you are about to go and meet one of those rare interviewers who really nails interviewing from the other side of the desk!

If you have little experience of interviewing others you will find looking over the Basic Backbone of a Structured Interview Process on page opposite particularly helpful.

In the sample process you can see how the various threads are grouped into a set of stages that help ensure the process is thorough and effective. This is just one example, albeit one we commonly experience. There is no perfect process, let alone a defined interview process. Many companies don't have a human resources department. It's not so much a question of the size of the company, more one of how much importance is attached to candidate selection as a means to achieve their objectives. Smaller companies who have paid a heavy price for getting hiring badly wrong will likely have a sturdier process than much bigger companies who have, for example, (perhaps through having a hiring authority or two with natural flair for sniffing out winners) avoided big mistakes.

But some order is better than none. Have a glance over the process outlined below and imagine as you do that you are the hiring authority – the individual who needs to add to their team.

BEFORE THE INTERVIEW
Select interview panel
Circulate job specification and CVs of shortlisted candidates
Pre-book interview dates and confirm availability
Brief panel members on areas for close scrutiny
Develop common questions (that will be asked of all candidates)

THE INTERVIEW
Nominate host to escort candidate while on premises and introduce
candidate to interviewer(s) (smaller companies won't delegate this)
60-minute slots – to take place on same day where possible
10-minute introduction to the interviewer, company and the specific role
20 minutes to ask questions
20 minutes to answer questions
10-minute wrap-up and any other business

POST-INTERVIEW(S)
Interviewer(s) submit independent feedback to HR
Interviewer(s) and HR (where applicable) meet to review and share
feedback on the candidate(s)
Select preferred candidate and alternative
Provide feedback to all and agree conclusion
Offer
Acceptance

POST-HIRE
Maintain contact during notice period (hiring manager)
Welcome and induct new hire to the company (HR)
Three-month review
Six-month probationary sign-off

The stages of this process could happen in one working day (except
post-hire of course), but more likely will be spread over a series of days,
weeks or even months.

THE THREE Ws

Essentially you really need to know the three Ws for each interview stage:

- **Who** are you meeting? Where do they sit in the decision-making process?
- **What** are they looking for? What is their style/approach?
- **Where** will you be meeting? What medium of communication will be used?

Let's take these Ws one at a time as we delve into what really happens to initiate, organise, deliver and review interview meetings, which forms the heartbeat of the hiring process.

WHO ARE YOU MEETING?

Who is conducting the interview? This could be an individual, one of a number of hiring authorities, an influencer (while not the actual decision maker, this is someone who is formally acknowledged as being part of the process and is influential in steering the outcome), an adviser or an assisting party (guest) to the process. Expect all sorts of planned and unplanned attendances:

- **One to one informal** – often referred to as a fireside chat. Usually used where there is not a formal vacancy, but there is a possibility of creating one; or where it is unlikely that the candidate wants (or even is able) to move now but the parties want to explore options well into the future.
- **One to one formal** – the most common interview format, usually used as part of a series of such meetings. Offers each side the most effective opportunity to assess the other fairly and objectively.
- **One to two** – tends to be used where the two people interviewing you actually do a lot of their day-to-day work together. In other instances the two-on-one is used to keep the process time down while allowing all of the parties to play their role.

- **One to many** – often set up as a conference or auditorium layout to provide a 'candidate on the stage' feel. You would usually be expected to present (for 10 to 20 minutes) and then field questions. It would not be fair to ask a candidate to do this without plenty of notice.
- **One to panel** – provides the opportunity for the quiet majority to pass judgement without ever having to involve themselves in active discourse. Imagine yourself seated in front of three to nine people who form a panel and being questioned by them in turn. Usually these sessions have a chairperson who runs the meeting and nominates who should speak when. Quite intimidating and pretty rare.
- **One to series** – on a single day you are shuffled from office to office. This model makes the best use of management time as in three to four hours they can all interview up to three candidates.
- **Super day/assessment day/gauntlet** – a large number of candidates are scheduled to attend on the same day and handled as a group. This is mostly used for graduate intake when looking to fill several trainee or apprenticeship slots during the year. It is rarely used above the trainee level. The opportunities to shine are matched by those to make mistakes, so while standing out is key you need to be remembered for the right reasons!
- **Trial half-day/day** – used in situations where the critical measure is seeing you in action on the job and among the colleagues you will work with.
- **Extended trial period** – a far more intensive version of the above. Can only be used when candidates are unemployed because you are unlikely to be able to do this if you are in a job.

Consider therefore the broader stakeholders. These are all the people either directly or indirectly linked to the role. The owners of the business are ultimately who you will work for. The manager hiring you is ultimately responsible to them for the decision to hire you or not.

Your ability to help that manager achieve their goals for the business flows up to their manager and so on to the very top.

THE COST OF HIRING MISTAKES

Hiring mistakes are very expensive. Most HR types know this well having either had a nasty experience first-hand or perhaps having wisely read Bradford D. Smart's *Topgrading: How Leading Companies Win by Hiring, Coaching and Keeping the Best People* (Portfolio, rev. ed., 2005), in which he calculates the real cost of hiring (a typical salesperson) at more than 20 times the annual salary of the candidate for a middle-order sales executive.

Imagine I am a plumber and I hire a young apprentice with a great attitude who indeed turns out to be excellent, remaining loyal to me for five years. During that time, I win 30 per cent more clients per annum (the clients like his attitude!) and we manage to get three additional strong employees to join (the workplace is made fun by his attitude!) – you get the gist of the importance of this hire to the company. Now imagine he had turned out to be a bad hire, who from the start cost me money but it takes me 18 months to exit him. The calculation is the difference between the win on the one hand and the loss on the other.

So interviewers need to try and hire the right person for the role in question first time. The interview processes we see today emerge from this pressure.

EVERYONE'S AN INTERVIEWER

Usually the interview process involves representatives from up and down the seniority chain by two or three levels. Each interviewer you meet as part of the process will have a slightly different relationship to the specific role you are being interviewed for.

The authority of HR and the way they use it varies markedly from one organisation to the next. In the extreme they can either proactively ease the passage of prospective candidates into the business or conversely present an impenetrable process wall that can feel like a hiring prevention machine. Either way, they deserve the same respect as anyone else you encounter in the process.

The personal assistants, receptionists and the periphery (all other roles impacted by the success or failure of the hire in question) are influencers. Some of these people could have a very significant impact on the final decision to go/not go with you as a hire.

It is safer and probably more accurate to take the view that *all* those employed by the company are interviewing you through a select band of nominated individuals on behalf of the shareholders/owners. Some more so than others, but ultimately everyone is motivated to make sure you are the right person for the role.

MAKE A GOOD IMPRESSION

I still feel a cold shiver when I recall a candidate of mine attending his first interview with a regional MD and being decidedly offhand and demeaning of the 'lowly' receptionist (as he apparently regarded her).

Unfortunately for him it transpired that her role twinned as executive assistant to the MD. No way was he going any further regardless of how much the MD liked him.

Be smart. You need to persuade them to want you for the job. Decision authority is supported by strong influence. You are being interviewed by everyone you meet so make a good impression on them all.

TYPES OF AUTHORITY

At any interview there are some obvious and essential details you should be given about the interviewer – name, title, etc. But in order to get a good grasp of who is conducting the interview you need to unpick where the individual fits within the business. This can be tricky in all but the smallest companies because an individual's authority, responsibility and influence is rarely linked to their title these days.

Furthermore, their title is not necessarily interdependent with other titles and designations around them. For simplicity's sake, when it comes to hiring decisions, it is best to focus on the question 'What authority do you hold?' This is a cheeky question, so it is not advisable to ask it as bluntly as this, rather keep it in mind and chip away for guidance where you can. You really could do with the answer.

If you have ever been on one of those interviews that is conducted by someone who has a flash title and acts the part, but the meeting that seemed promising simply dissolves to nothing and you never really know why, then you might have some sympathy for this notion.

In reality there are just three key types of authority:

- Hierarchical
- Delegated
- Earned

Each of these describes a different sort of animal, so ideally you would have some inkling as to the sort you are destined to meet.

Hierarchical Authority
The hierarchical leadership structure of almost all companies tends to look like the classic pyramid model you will find adopted in organisations large and small. From the armed forces, through public-sector bodies to blue-chip companies and on into the mid- and small-cap companies. We are all touched by this structure to some extent.

Contemporary attempts to demonstrate a shift away from the classic models have resulted in a variety of fads, but in reality 'flat' (where most management layers are eliminated to bring the workers close to a few senior decision makers; based on the notion that well-trained workers will be more productive if they are given direct input to the decision making along with a high level of trust) and 'matrix' (where skills are pooled and then delivered to projects as and when required under specific project-leadership teams who have to win the loyalty of the people they need to deliver their project) models are typically applied to various elements such as projects, programmes and pursuit initiatives within an overall pyramid-style structure as opposed to being applicable to the whole enterprise. Don't let loose descriptions such as 'We run a very flat management model here' give you the impression that the CEO is now peer to the cleaner. They are not!

Ultimately when it comes to who is involved on the selection panel for a given role the determining factor will likely be time. If the CEO of the company had unlimited time then for sure they would like to be involved in every interview across the entire business at every level. That way they could be certain that the quality thresholds they would like to see upheld are indeed maintained with no exceptions. However, they don't have unlimited time. So the CEO sets the bar for quality as defined by their own metric and then they hire leaders to whom they delegate. This delegation cascades down in a managed way to enable each level to deliver within available time constraints.

Does your interviewer have authority as a result of their hierarchical status? Do they also command respect? Have they earned it?

Delegated Authority

Consider the warehouse shift leader who is asked by their boss to stand in as overall head of the warehouse while he is away on holiday; the financial controller asked to assume the financial director's responsibility when their boss is unexpectedly unable to work through illness. From such temporary delegations come opportunities for sharing or winning authority; for aspirations to grow.

Usually delegated authority exists where people are trusted and empowered to get on with their jobs without the need to defer, check and ask permission at every juncture. The control mechanisms exist but so too does trust.

Does your interviewer have delegated authority? Are they empowered by a confident sponsor to get on with their job?

Earned Authority

The warehouse shift leader and the financial controller I just mentioned have done so well with the authority temporarily delegated to them that they are now trusted to get on with much of the decision making of their bosses because they have earned trust. They have earned authority.

Within the ranks of such people lies the true power base of great companies. It is these individuals who can:

- Resolve disputes.
- Sniff trouble long before it has fully developed into material and significant issues.
- Manage big egos.
- Communicate difficult or bad news to workers and manage the fallout.
- Ask for the extra mile from the team for little or nothing in return.
- Convince a cynical client that the business really does care about the contract and how it is delivered.

In addition to these many attributes they can also pick winning candidates from those shortlisted.

The people I am referring to here are not the shop steward or union representative. Rather, these are individuals who are looked up to by their colleagues and their management as people leaders.

Has your interviewer got the real authority of one who has truly earned it?

DIG DEEP FOR INFORMATION

It is essential these days to enter the interviewer's name into an Internet search engine and see what you can find out about them. They will *expect* you to have done this basic level of preparation. But *dig deeper*. If you are really determined to find out about your interviewer you are going to have to do a little more research. Most of what you need to know is not going to be in the public domain, however: use LinkedIn to find a recent leaver from the company you're interviewing at. Contact them via InMail or be brave and call them up: 'Hi, this is Tim Vincent, we haven't spoken before, I'll be brief. I am interviewing with ABC Inc. and I notice from your LinkedIn records that you recently left the company. Would you mind if I picked your brains for a minute or two?' I guarantee you they will ask: 'Who are you interviewing with?' And there's your opening.

WHAT ARE THEY LOOKING FOR?

In the typical interview process you will encounter all three types of authority. It helps greatly to know, or at least have a feel for, which type you are working with as their approach to the interview will be very different. Here are the headline characteristics for each.

Hierarchical

Think of the long termer who has worked their way up the ranks the hard way and doesn't particularly like anyone finding shortcuts around them. Respects process and order.

Looks for: A traditionalist? Likely to prefer to hire to the specification and let the organisation itself sort the wheat from the chaff. Tends to dislike the overambitious and those younger and far more capable than themselves. Likely to opt to grow talent from within the company, so prefers the product of the graduate intake over the headhunted rock stars.

Delegated

As above, but with less time served. Has managed to accumulate more authority than their position naturally carries. In this group are the very capable yet under-promoted, who take on additional responsibility but without the benefit of the trappings (bigger title, higher designation, higher earnings, etc.). They have the expectation that progression and promotion will come through diligent service and loyalty.

Looks for: Hard workers. Probably happier measuring inputs and effort as opposed to outputs and earnings. So will seek out those of the same ilk and will be impressed by those who win with strategies linked to principles of hard work.

Earned

Has the skill, flair, ambition and confidence to progress on merit alone. Likely to enjoy the support of management a tier or two above in the hierarchy. Possibly marked out for bigger things (though these individuals also split opinion as they break hierarchical rules and conformist norms so will have their detractors) and always looking for the steps that can help them get there.

Looks for: Flair. There is no obvious measure for entrepreneurial flair and you cannot know whether someone will be lucky for you (and themselves). However, these individuals will be the most likely to believe that they have the Midas touch. They look for rule breakers who win; shortcut takers who have earned the right not to have to follow the processes, strictures and norms, rather they do whatever it takes to win.

Preparing for and handling each of these different authority types is more about having the courage of your convictions and not making changes to your natural approach than preparing specifically for a type.

If you tell a professional golfer in advance that they are going to play a course where the greens are fast, the fairways are slow and the bunkers are unforgiving, do you think they change their golf swing on the first tee? No. The swing always remains the same regardless of the conditions. However, they take this information on board. Out on the course they would adapt based on their own findings and perhaps bear reference to the information you gave them. Ultimately, those with the most swing conviction will likely be among the highest achievers on the professional tour.

So, the point of the golfing analogy is to tell you to have the courage of your convictions.

WHAT AND WHO DO THEY WANT?

I don't think you will be surprised to learn that our clients struggle when we delve into the deeper reaches of what they really want to hire and how they will know that the right candidate is sat in front of them. They just hadn't thought of the role or what the ideal candidate for it might look like from all of the angles we need to. Most often they simply know that they:

- Have headcount (approved capacity to hire one or more people).
- Have the budget.
- Have a vacancy.
- Need to fill the role or risk not delivering on or above target performance against their own metrics.
- Have a team that has the great, the good, the mediocre and the poor represented in it and they would like to add to the great and the good.

Sometimes they will fancy themselves as naturally good talent spotters: 'I just know them when I see them so show me some candidates.' Others are at the analytical end of the spectrum: 'Please help me to narrow down precisely what we ought to aim for here.'

Then there is every type in between too.

If you have a job specification for a role you are applying for now please pull it out, otherwise try to get hold of one from your archives.

Failing either of these options, reach for your keyboard and search for 'job specification' to give you a feel for an example or two.

Now do a quick comparison between the Search Order form (see pages 83–86) and the specification in your hand. You will almost certainly find several key gaps in areas that relate to:

- **Personality**: Job specs are a little like a coat of varnish over the real thing. They skimp on the detail of what is really required to avoid the risk of offending anyone.
- **Performance**: At the heart of the matter is what the business needs done by this newcomer and how this will be measured and rewarded. Again difficult to describe at the varnish layer.
- **Preference**: Why should a great person join at this time is usually lost in hyperbole about the company generally – 'ABC has a global footprint boasting 15,000 staff' – this is not a reason to join them!

So treat any and all job specs with suspicion.

What people *say* they want and what they *really* want are often very different things. These specification documents just don't tend to get to the heart of the matter. They don't describe the person they really want to hire, rather they gloss over the role description in an impersonal manner that makes them highly misleading.

It is very likely that before you are offered a job, and indeed before you are certain you want to take up any role, you will go through more than one interview. We typically expect at least two, and often up to four, separate visits will be required, though ten is not unknown!

There aren't any generally applied rules, regulations or stipulations about the interview process, rather it is at the discretion of two primary bodies:

1. **The organisation and their human resource guidelines**
   For example, ACME Holdings Inc. might have a current policy that all candidates for roles at all levels are interviewed by three people – one at the same grade as the job on offer and one from each of the two grades above.

2. **The hiring authority for the particular role you are applying for**

Let's say that the warehouse manager for ACME Logistics Ltd might value the personal insight of one particular individual whom he worked with previously in another division. He therefore personally sees to it that this individual is brought in to help interview the final shortlist of candidates.

So although you might hear someone espousing one particular interview process over another, it is worth bearing in mind that there is no formal best practice for agreeing how a candidate to hire is chosen, rather it is a discretionary deal. I hesitate to use the phrase 'best candidate' since what this phrase means is of course open to interpretation and immediately touches on one of the biggest headaches for any organisation seeking to hire, namely: 'How do the interested parties agree on what it is we want to hire?' followed by 'How do we agree on how best we go about finding it?'

Yes, there are bodies (usually human resources led) that have tried to standardise what they see as best practice. The Chartered Institute of Personnel and Development (CIPD) is one such. You will find that in organisations that allow HR to govern with an iron fist there is some rigid structure enforced that all must follow. However, this is not the norm outside of the Fortune 500 (the world's largest companies).

HOW THEY GET WHAT THEY WANT

Regardless of how the interview process is settled on, there are a number of options available to those interested in ensuring they hire good candidates. Consider the following selection of commonly applied tools of the trade. Bear in mind as you read through this list that under any and all scrutiny, you having the confidence of your convictions is more important than any tips of mine.

Trial sessions

Inviting you to spend a trial day working with your prospective employers places you under the scrutiny of the whole team. In short, the number of interviewers just grew by a significant number, widening the possibility that someone won't warm to you.

On such days many of your future colleagues get the opportunity to get to know you and will form part of the meeting that discusses your fit for the role in question. These trial sessions are usually more about how you behave, fit in, adapt and react within the team than they are about any specific achievements during the short period of the session.

Tip: What a wonderful opportunity for you to interview them. Such 'sheep-dip' techniques (where you are literally dropped into the team to emerge on the other side with a good understanding on both sides of your relative fit) come in a variety of forms. The two-way assessment and 'get to know you' naturally develops to a much more intimate level at which you can gain a far more accurate feel of what it is really like to work in the company. Relish the opportunity to be curious (people like people who are interested in them), empathetic (people like people who are like them) and positive (people like people who like them) among the team.

Two or more on one

This is when interviewers who you weren't expecting to see are added to the meeting. These extras are often briefed to look for particular traits and instead of asking questions will often sit through all or just part of the meeting as observers.

There is merit in this tactic in so far as two views are better than one. When you are conducting an interview you can miss a lot of important traits, characteristics and specifics that a fellow interviewer might pick up loud and clear simply because they were looking for them and were not distracted by leading the meeting.

Tips: Address yourself to the interview panel as a whole. Avoid the risk of narrowing your attention to one or other of the interviewers regardless of whom the questions are coming from. Treat the panel as a collective and look each of them in the eye in turn as you speak. By all means prefer the individual who has asked you the question, but take care to address the others too – you need to know you have everyone's attention, all of the time.

Ask a question or two of those interviewers who sit the quietest. They will be flattered and kept engaged – an easy win.

Keep asking yourself 'Have I got them all with me?' The interviewers know this can be an unsettling format. This actually gives you a little room to have a few nerves so in fact the meeting is usually more balanced as a result.

Prepared presentations

'Please prepare a twenty-minute formal presentation entitled "My first ninety days at ABC Inc." and using any media you like on the day you will be invited to deliver this presentation to a maximum of five attendees.' This is a typical example of what you might be asked to prepare for an interview presentation.

Even if you know that presenting is not your strong suit it needn't reflect badly on you provided your preparation is well managed. Knowing what it is you want to say and actually having it scripted is more than half the challenge. Don't set yourself the double challenge of making it up and presenting it in the same instance – that is the domain of the world's leading stand-up comics only.

Beginning: Grab the audience's attention right away, being a little dramatic is best: 'The YouTube video "United Breaks Guitars" goes viral and knocks 5 per cent off United's stock price. How on earth do we control this social-media animal? I have twenty minutes to share some views on this. Do feel free to interrupt with any questions.' This opening is way better than: 'I'd like to share some observations about the Internet and its impact on global businesses for twenty minutes. For my first slide I have a graph that …' This isn't going to engage anyone. Another effective way to begin is with a challenging question, to which you are going to present the answer, or at least have a good attempt at doing so.

Middle: Make your examples and references as relevant to the audience as possible. Use real case studies that touch the people in the room where you can. Be brave and give your own impressions, interpretations, forecasts and vision of the future as opposed to simply passing on the views of others.

End: Finish with a flourish that will leave them wanting more: 'I'm going to round up now and pass over to you for questions. However, before I do there is a headline question that I feel jumps out – "What does this mean to ABC today?" and I would like briefly to tackle this while you consider any questions that you might have.'

Using visual aids to get your message across is something you should only do having checked in advance that it is either expected or preferred. In many cases it is frowned upon as there have been countless misuses of slide decks. Many a seasoned interviewer literally turns off the moment the laptop or iPad is turned on. If you do use PowerPoint keep the following three points in mind:

1. Keep the deck to just a few informative slides (two to three minutes per slide).
2. Print three copies of the deck and take a memory stick with the presentation stored on it with you (don't lean too heavily on technology – it can let you down). For three people or less just hand out the printed version rather than using your laptop or a projector. This is more intimate because they then have their own version of your presentation that combines as a 'takeaway'.
3. Don't read what is on the slide, rather provide embellishment and colour to your displayed bullet points.

If you intend to use a projector or any other display equipment then it's your responsibility to make sure it will be there and that it is in working order. Book it well in advance and call the day before the interview to check that everything will be ready.

Tip: The beauty of the prepared presentation is that you have time to get yourself ready and to practise. I suggest you find someone who has some public-speaking experience and ask them to sit and listen to your presentation. Oddly, most people find this much harder than the real thing. Your presentation will improve exponentially with each delivery and the real thing will be a breeze in comparison.

Role-play simulations

Here's a clichéd example of what you might be asked to do: 'If you imagine for a moment you are a stationery sales executive, please could you try to sell me this pencil.'

Tip: The trick is in the questions you ask. If you are thrown into role play with no preparation you have every reason to ask for a little more detail. I'll use the pencil example to show you what I mean.

Put the pencil in your pocket as you think about what questions to ask to gain the information that you need to know. For example, you could ask: 'When you buy stationery how do you know quality?' 'Can I get a feel for your annual needs for writing and drawing instruments?' 'What number of people do you tend to source for?' 'Ever use ballpoints that fail?'

So you can see by focusing on questions I have got beyond that brain freeze of 'How do I sell this pencil? Eeek!' It is far easier to think, 'What do I need to know and how do I ask for it?' The majority of role play is handled by questions that clarify and inform.

They don't really need you to sell them the pencil. They are interested in how you develop the situation to the point where you might be able to influence them to buy something – from ideas, to services to products. So you just need to get really interested in them.

Assessment centre

Invite all who pass the basic threshold to attend a meeting venue either on the company premises or, more commonly, off-site. This usually replaces the first interview and therefore acts as a collective first interview for all of the candidates who would have earned a one-to-one interview were there fewer of them. This format is much favoured by HR departments tasked with sifting the wheat from the chaff.

Once all are assembled the usual approach is to run a series of collective comparison exercises. Here are a few exercises that are often used:

- In tray – usually an individual exercise. Each of the candidates is given a tray or folder containing the same documents. You are usually also given a set of verbal notes of additional things that have come up that you must bear in mind. The objective of the exercise is to prioritise the written and verbal tasks quickly and explain how you arrived at the order you feel you should tackle things in.

- Group problem solving – divided into teams, you are presented with a problem and you will need to present your solution to the other teams who will critique your findings.
- Case study – you are given a case study – usually based upon a serious incident, such as an airline disaster – and asked to present two or three immediate fixes that would help ensure it wasn't repeated.
- Team forming/norming – one or more business games involving different props that challenge aspects such as your memory, creativity, humour, communication skills and arithmetic abilities.

The use of assessment centres is much favoured by HR departments. They sit back and watch the action unfold, assess the candidates together and watch the cream rise to the top. The dynamics of the group reveal aspects that are difficult to spot one on one.

Tips: You might think that there is no scope to prepare for this type of day since you simply can't predict what will happen, however, you can and should:

1. Sharpen your current affairs awareness by watching/reading the news.
2. Hone your wit by mingling with friends and strangers. Don't spend the two days prior to the assessment in lonely isolation as the shock of parachuting into a room with a lot of people you don't know may make you freeze.
3. Play games, complete puzzles and try a little creative thinking with a friend or partner. Start with noughts and crosses and go from there. One trick that helps is to think up new rules as you go along or try inventing a whole new game. Another option is to get the Lego out of the cupboard and set yourself a challenge such as, 'I have thirty seconds to assemble these

twenty pieces into something you can name – no actions or sounds allowed.'

There are some guiding principles that do help on the day itself:

1. Make a big effort to mingle and interact with as many people as possible.
2. Listen very carefully to instructions and preferably make notes to be sure.
3. Volunteer whenever invited to.
4. Lead, guide and assist whenever you have the opportunity to.

In collective interview sessions such as this the decision to hire becomes homogenised between the interview team, the candidates (self-selection) and the many facets of the intensive group process. The interview team as a whole, and individual members of the team, thereby avoid being suckered into missing a key aspect or trait and making a hiring mistake.

WHERE WILL YOU BE MEETING?

Location, format and media play an important role in setting the tone for the meeting. These factors have a significant bearing on the perceptions and impressions you form of each other. So it is not surprising that where you find employers working hard to attract talent you see them taking great care to ensure that candidates get the right impression, whereas in situations in which workers are over-supplied you find employers being far less diligent. The bottom line is that a candidate's thought prior to an interview will be: 'Do these people respect me enough to roll out any kind of carpet?'

Media	Pros, cons, dos and don'ts
Telephone You will be connected to your interviewer for voice only. Typically for 30–45 minutes. Usually used by HR or the admin. department for checking details. Not usually a format used by hiring authorities unless there is no other option available (e.g where time and distance necessitate).	**Pro**: Time efficient as both interviewer and candidate just have to find a private space with a landline telephone (I recommend you don't rely on your mobile phone unless you can be certain of the signal). **Con**: Voice is only a small (albeit key) part of communication. Telephone meetings precede but cannot replace face-to-face meetings. So okay for some of the meetings in a wider process but for both parties it is essential to meet in person. **Do**: Use inflection and what is not said, i.e. implied through tone, volume, pace and variety, to add impact and colour. When you practise try delivering your prompt sheets (see pages 78 and 139) over the phone. Keep it sharp and clipped. Imagine you need to keep the interviewer awake and with you throughout. **Don't**: Get caught in a monotone or speak for too long before allowing the other person to speak.
Video conference The next best thing to meeting in person. Now much more commonplace as the technology has come down in price.	**Pro**: Again, time efficient as there is likely a suite near to you and the interviewer. I don't think Voice over Internet Protocol (VoIP), such as Skype, is the right service to use for this purpose. The bandwidth somewhere between the two of you will affect the call. Bespoke solutions such as Tandberg are exceptional and can substitute for, though not completely replace, a face-to-face meeting. **Con**: You are talking to a TV! There is something detached and impersonal about the experience. However good the connection you are missing the physical shaking of hands that bookends the face to face, the eyeball to eyeball and the pouring and drinking of tea! **Do**: Keep your body movements quiet. There is often a lag between the video and voice signals, which can be distracting and is hugely enhanced if you are jumping around. Maintain direct eye contact with the lens.

Media	Pros, cons, dos and don'ts
	Don't: Read too much into the interviewer's behaviour. Sometimes their behaviour may appear lazy or even rude, such as them typing or not looking at you. They won't be like this when you finally meet face to face. It isn't personal, rather a symptom of the misuse of technology.
Face to face Befitting of the importance of the meeting and preferred where practical. Almost always timed to 60 minutes, though there are no rules!	**Pro**: The ideal format for human beings to assess each other. Our senses naturally evolved over millions of years in part to help us handle these types of encounters. The body signals and what is not said are at least as important as what is more obviously communicated. By having prepared exceptionally well to nail the interview you can relax and focus more intently on these critical signals and messages to help ensure you better understand the individual you are meeting with.
	Con: There is no hiding place. Nerves, uncertainty and character flaws are all more visible in this setting.
	Do: Believe. Now that you have prepared to nail the interview you are ready for this meeting. So 'wear' the right attitude. It is here that 'Do I want the job?' has so much more weight than 'Persuade them to want me for the job'.
	Don't: Be late for the meeting. You can undermine world-class presentation by simply missing a bus or getting stuck in a traffic jam. The interviewer could legitimately say, 'If you can't organise travel logistics for an important meeting to get you here on time how can I have any confidence that you will be able to hold meaningful responsibility?'

Regardless of how many people are involved in interviewing you, how formal the structure, ordered the venue, pressurised or relaxed the approach, the backbone to the interview preparation and delivery laid out in the steps remains *the same*.

Your interview preparation should improve through the process as you get more insight into the company and people you are interviewing with.

STEP 7: RESEARCH THE ROLE – KEY POINTS

- More information now = Less needed at interview = More time.
- What is the role? Use the headhunter's Search Order form to help you understand what you need to know before the interview.
- What is the selection process?
- Take a look from the interviewer's perspective to gain insight into the hiring process and practices of which the interview forms a key part.
- Use the basic backbone of a structured interview as a starting point.
- The three Ws:
  - Who are you meeting?
  - What are they looking for?
  - Where will you be meeting?

STEP 8: READY YOUR ANSWERS

A balanced interview will see you fielding questions from the interviewer. You might as well face it … the questions are coming! Whatever they ask you, you need to respond and you need to respond well. I'm not going to give you stock answers that you just regurgitate. I'm going to help you by arming you with:

1. The right **attitude**.
2. A simple **framework** for responding to *any* question.

ATTITUDE

Caring about the consequences of failure can so undermine your attempts to succeed that unfortunately rejection can be self-fulfilling. At the other extreme, cockiness and overconfidence are likely to lead to the same outcome − rejection. You need to arm yourself with the right attitude. Attitude armour can be put on like your clothes. Think to yourself:

'I only really need and want this job if it is right for me at this time.'

This should be your attitude. You are entering the interview to carry out diligence on whether or not this is the right career platform for you, *not* to get a yes at all costs. The yeses will come as a product of your attitude. Your attitude armour combined with the steps you have followed in this book will make you a formidable candidate. Perhaps you might even prefer the somewhat more aggressive thought:

> *'I really don't need this job unless the interviewer can convince me it is right for my career.'*

TWO TRUTHS

Here are two truths that once you really accept them will help you wear the right attitude all the time.

TRUTH NO. 1: NO FROM YOU IS OKAY

I am sure that your interview will be productive. If, however, you do find yourself realising that the role isn't for you or indeed the wheels really come off and you find yourself playing a part in someone else's whacky and bizarre cartoon, then I suggest that your answer to your foundation question – 'Do I want the job? – is simply – no! So at least in this regard the weird meeting was effective since it left you in no doubt about what your decision would be.

Just move on. Your preparedness to say no is half of the attitude armour you will wear on the day. It is half of what makes you an attractive candidate.

TRUTH NO. 2: NO FROM THE INTERVIEWER IS OKAY

Ultimately, however well you use the steps in this book, there will probably be interviews you attend where the response from the interviewer is 'no'. They do not want to hire you for the job.

A 'no' from the interviewer is good. Really it is. Welcome that chance to explore the boundaries of your career options and welcome all that you learn from the feedback (which you will probably need to push for as many interviewers are used to giving very simple one-liners and you could use more than that). I can assure you with total conviction that if you use these steps and don't get through a particular interview doorway then that was not the ideal route for your career at that time.

These steps were not designed to get you accepted into *any* job. This is a ludicrous idea as it implies you should apply for a role you simply cannot and should not win yet expect to get offered the job regardless. They were designed to help ensure that, given the chance to interview for it, you *do get* the best next step in your career offered to you so that you can choose to accept it if that is what you want to do.

The interviewer who said no was right. You will find in time that you don't actually need that job, rather the closed door moves you on down the corridor a door or two and the one you do knock on will be opened wide because of what you have learnt from those earlier experiences.

CAP RESPONSE FRAMEWORK

You have the right attitude, so now you need a framework to help you respond well to the interview questions. The principle for good question handling in all types of interview meetings is to remember CAP: check, ask, present.

- **C**heck to make sure you understand the question by ensuring you test your understanding. This is an important and powerful ploy because it is far easier to respond to a question that checks your understanding than to actually answer the question.
- **A**sk yourself 'How do I use that question to illustrate my achievements?'
- **P**resent your answer in an illustrative and compelling way. We'll look at how and why you can be assured that your response will be strong.

Let's see how CAP works in practice.

CAP – CHECK

Consider the question:

'What is the worst mistake you feel you have made in your professional career thus far?'

This is a really nasty, curve ball of a question that a clever human resources officer no doubt dreamt up when they were on a mission to pin down an overconfident candidate who needed to be brought down a peg or two. I'm not joking. By the way, I am giving you a question at the more extreme end of the scale because, after all, the title of this book is *Nail That Interview* not *Interview Okay*!

Don't imagine that the questions that get thrown at you emerge from a special interview-question lab. No, the majority come from the minds of interviewers who can be in any one of an infinite number of moods. These are people doing their jobs; working on behalf of colleagues, stakeholders, companies, corporations and shareholders.

They are people who have been on your side of the desk, too. They are people just like you and me. Behind the facade of these crazy questions in this weird meeting is a *real* person. That is the person you *really* need to meet!

So if I asked you to simply qualify the question as opposed to searching your memory for an appropriate answer then you might respond with:

'By mistake do you mean where I feel I have fallen short of what I wanted to achieve performance wise or where I actually made a wrong turn in terms of career decision making?'

Or perhaps alternatively something simpler still:

'We all make mistakes. I have learnt from plenty of them. What sort of mistake are you looking for here?'

All you have had to do is redefine the question and push it back at the interviewer. It's far easier to do this than to actually answer the question with a single response and it achieves two important things:

- **Evens up the control**: You are showing the interviewer that you are not simply going to answer their questions, rather you are going to make absolutely sure you know what they want and you are going to aim to provide it to them in a considered way. The big trap that turns the majority of candidates into quivering heaps of mediocrity is falling into a Q&A, Q&A, Q&A pattern ... question – answer, question – answer, question – answer ...

> Q. Who is in control of the meeting?
> A. The person asking the questions!

So each question deserves at least a qualifier in exchange to even things up. We don't do subservience to interviewers – we level the playing field.

- **Allows you time**: You will have a little breathing space to ask yourself 'How do I use that question to illustrate my achievements?'

IDENTIFYING WEAKNESSES

To complement the CAP framework you need to be very brutal with yourself as to those areas of your capability and fit that could be seen as weaknesses. Please don't fall into the trap of assuming that your weaknesses are those cliché areas that you need to churn out when prompted. No, we are looking here for the chinks in your armour that are well hidden but that a determined interviewer can get at. Your strengths more than compensate I am sure, but we need to look for the hidden weakness within. Here are some examples that might present as a strength and then when analysed reveal a weakness:

- A preparedness to cut corners when time dictates.
- A ruthless streak that sees you win but at some cost to your relationship with those who trust you and rely on you.
- A shyness that you compensate for by talking a lot so people perceive you as assured and confident.
- Team successes attributed to you that had a good dose of luck about them.

📖 Turn to a new page in your journal and write the heading 'My Weaker Points'.

Take the five key competency criteria for the role you are interviewing for and consider how a critical interviewer will measure you against them.

Usually you will be able to pick the top five criteria out of the role specification if it is reasonably clear. It should highlight the 'must haves' or 'critical experience' and these will be good pointers to what they consider the most important aspects. Imagine you are the interviewer and your task is simply to hire just to the written specification. Break it down into headline points and select what you feel emerge as the top five criteria.

Next we need to weigh you against these criteria using a very critical eye (unreasonably harsh is good for the purposes of this exercise) and I suggest you mark yourself out of 10 using the following guide:

Criteria scoring guide	
10	Exceed the credentials for the criteria by a clear margin. Will easily fulfil immediate and foreseen requirements. Overqualification might be a challenge?
7–9	Meet all and exceed some of the credentials for the criteria. Will likely cope with immediate and foreseen requirements but not overqualified.
5–6	Meet some of the credentials for the criteria but not all and in some cases short of the required level.
2–4	Meet few if any of the credentials for the criteria but in some cases will have the ability with training and support to step up to most or even all.
1	Meet none of the credentials for the criteria and unlikely to be able to cover or fill the gap even with training.

Now have a go at assessing how you measure up against the top five criteria. Here is an example to help give you an idea of what the end result should look like:

Criteria	My score	How does the critical interviewer unpick me on this one?
Specific engineering experience.	**2/10** I have not taken my career down a thoroughbred engineering track.	They will ask me specifically how much engineering experience I have and then will dig for examples. They will ask for dates and durations.
Turn around a failing team.	**6/10** Yes, but not in the sales arena nor in engineering.	They will ask what experience of turnaround I have and will want to know how it was I achieved success in this. Likely they will ask about sales–engineering fit.
Degree qualified.	**1/10** I pulled out of my degree course and have never completed it.	They will ask 'Why did you pull out of your degree course?' They will stress that a degree is preferred and ask me 'Why do you think this might be important?'
Leadership credentials.	**7/10** I think a stronger suit. I have always been seen as a leader.	They will explore my leadership experience and in particular will expect me to be honest about mistakes I've learnt along the way – no one is perfect.
Good communicator and presenter.	**5/10** I am better one on one, though do have presenting experience.	They will ask me to present to them and perhaps a small group of others on a relevant topic. They will ask me to explain how and why I feel I am good one on one.

Now that you have acknowledged these you have already begun to equip yourself to manage the inevitable questions that a good interviewer will pose.

HOW DO INTERVIEWERS CHOOSE WHICH QUESTIONS TO ASK?

So what's behind the trickiest questions? Where do they come from? How are they formed? Let's have a look at how good interviewers brief themselves ahead of the meeting as a means of gaining some insight.

Basics

A sound knowledge of the marketplace within which their business operates is essential. Knowledge of the pond is as key for the employer as it is for the employee/candidate. The more thorough the understanding of the bullseye the better aim they can take and the higher their hit ratio.

Tip: Be aware of and manage your reputation in your bullseye. Make the publicity good publicity wherever you can. All publicity will precede you into a well-run process.

CV dissection

Most interviewers assume (rightly in most cases) that there is a degree of embellishment and exaggeration contained in CVs and don't stop hunting until they have tracked it down. There are sleuth organisations that specialise in weeding out such things.

Tip: Be honest in your CV. Don't leave gaps and ensure that dates are accurate.

Advance reference points

Because they have your CV, the interviewer will know where you work and may try to gain some inside information on you by calling someone at your current workplace. This needs to be done very discreetly as it's a dangerous move for both parties. It's safe to assume that the interviewer will probably be given some negative comments about you from these insiders whether or not they have any substance.

Tip: There is no need to make enemies of people whom you don't perhaps like. Focus on courting success in your career then if people speak ill of you it will be more than tempered by those who support and praise you.

Behavioural psychometrics

What is your Myers Briggs score? What about your SelecSys or P6? I don't expect you will be familiar with all or even any of these terms, but in the world of recruitment these are commonplace tools for character and behaviour assessment. In responding to a set of questions that you complete (usually online), the interviewer will be provided with a comparison between the way you completed the test relative to all others who have completed it to form a perspective on the primary traits of your character.

Shortly after arrival for an interview you may be asked to complete a 30 to 90-minute multiple-choice exercise, the results of which will then be used during your interview. At an appropriate point in the meeting the interviewer will likely refer to this graph in a manner that implies that they can, through this information, see into your soul. While this sort of information ought to be treated with great care by trained interpreters who have learnt to balance the output carefully with what they find through normal interview discourse, unfortunately it is usually wholly misused by people with only a notional grasp of what the output means and who then attach far too much weight to a specific psychometric scoreline.

Tip: Fill these tests out honestly as an account of how you reflect on yourself today. There is a simple algorithm in most of these software-based tests that picks up anomalies and provides a 'test integrity' score. This integrity test will, if it registers issues of contradiction or lack of consistency to a large enough degree, probably be sufficient to invalidate the whole test if you have tried a little too hard to present yourself as someone you are not.

Aptitude testing

This usually involves a set of arithmetic- or logic-based questions that are geared to the specific role that you are interviewing for.

You either know the answers or you don't. If you don't, then you don't. There is scope where the test is not multiple choice to at least express your thinking as to how you might arrive at the answer. They always told you at school to show your workings and actually the wrong answer with the right workings can get you the mark because that is what some of these tests look for.

If the interviewer requires that you do know the answers (i.e. they are placing critical weighting on the aptitude testing) then this role is probably not for you and you can use the interview to explore other possibilities. Rarely, and usually only in highly technical roles – e.g.

engineering, sciences, medicine and areas of finance – are such tests critical deciders as to whether or not you proceed or are rejected.

Tip: If you are going to have an aptitude test, make sure that you bone up on the basics. I have lost count of the number of candidates who have kicked themselves after one of these tests because they couldn't recall one of the elementary basics they hadn't used for ages and yet used to take for granted. Just get out the textbooks and remind yourself. Each page of the textbook you look at, ask yourself: 'What question could they ask me about this?'

CAP – ASK AND PRESENT

This section is about *ask* and *present* from the CAP framework, about getting from the question to your FAB (see pages 71–74). So, 'How do I use that question to illustrate my achievements?' could be rephrased as 'How do I get from that question to one of my stories?' You might well have seen politicians use this approach:

Journalist: Minister, what do you say to the hard-working families up and down the country who now cannot afford to pay for heating oil since your tax hikes have pressed the price beyond them?

Minister: Since this government came to office we have eased the pressure on the purse of the working family while asking those who can afford it to do their bit. More money on schools, more on fighting crime, more on health and more to help people back to work. For the truly needy we have set more money aside for allowances and tax credits.

Recognise this? The minister didn't really answer the question – they used it as a springboard to say something they wanted to get across. In my view they abuse this too, but that doesn't make it a bad tool. On the contrary, in an interview this is an essential tool!

You should use the opportunity to answer where you can with one of your stories to provide an illustrated response in an entertaining way, all the time loading your FAB detail into the interviewer's memory.

This is a simple and effective tool that you can use and, with just a little practice, it's one at which you can become proficient. Here is how it looks in practice:

Interviewer: What is the worst mistake you feel you have made in your professional career thus far?

You: We all make mistakes. I have learnt from plenty of them. What sort of mistake are you looking for here?

Interviewer: Oh – just the worst one!

You: Okay. Well, actually what springs to mind is me holding up my hand to take on a big challenge. No one else stepped up when the MD asked for volunteers to respond to the BG invitation to tender. After all, we had bid and lost it three times before so why would this time be any different? That initial mistake of putting my hand in the air landed me with six months of hard yards for no obvious reward. So the account landed in my lap and I figured I might as well give it my best shot. I decided to turn that mistake around. I called the head of the process and asked for an extension as we were already behind. He was actually very appreciative. We struck up a great relationship that resulted ultimately in our winning what would become one of the largest accounts in Europe.

So my mistake did have a happy ending I guess. But I have to say I am more cautious now when it comes to volunteering because I am better at pre-qualifying what I work on to ensure I keep a high win ratio.

TYPICAL INTERVIEW QUESTIONS

Here are some more examples of questions that interviewers sprinkle into the typical interview. I have provided example answers that draw on the CAP and FAB approaches from candidates up and down the spectrum, all of whom have applied the same simple rules.

Rather than concentrating on the actual content of the answer, focus on the structure and use of CAP and FAB. As you read through them pick out both techniques and begin to consider how you would respond with your own answer that exploits these powerful tools. (I – interviewer, C – candidate.)

Example 1

I: Why are you looking to leave your current school to come and teach for us?

C: Actually it's not that I am looking to leave my teaching job, rather that I'm interested in career advancement and from what I can gather St Cuthberts is well placed to offer me good prospects for this. What do you feel it is about this school that works best at the moment and conversely what do you feel you need to aim to improve in the short term?'

Example 2

I: What makes you a good department manager for a mid-size retailer?

C: I hope my results speak for themselves. Should I just outline how I managed to outperform all of the other regions by 20 per cent year on year?

I: Sure. That would be interesting.

C: Firstly I haven't been in charge of pulling people in or footfall – that is for marketing, but I have owned conversion once they are across the threshold and I think the best illustration of my laser focus on this is a recent customer visit. Jane and her three young children came into the shoe department and I could see she was in a hurry so I said 'Excuse me but I can see you are in a hurry – perhaps if you give me a steer I can sort your shoe needs in a flash!' She smiled a little and then gave me a list of requirements – most of which were clothing and food, but some of which were school shoes. So I said 'Best if I take quick shoe sizes for each of them and then you go and round up the rest of your shopping while I lay out all of the best options for when you return in an hour from now. Long story short she bought two pairs of shoes for each child and a pair for herself. But the real net of this customer service was that she sent four of her friends with families in later that day in exchange for an extra discount I offered her and them. How much latitude do you allow your department managers to drive the P&L?

Example 3

I: What makes you a great clothes designer?

C: In terms of creative inspiration, originality or commercial success – how do you judge greatness?

I: Hmmm. Good question. Let's go with commercial success since that is how I am driven after all.

C: I don't allow the other two to run away with me such that I fail to realise the last and ultimately most important criterion. We begin achieving commercial success by knowing what our clients want to buy and part of that is drawn each year from what shapes, styles and colours they see on the catwalk and in the celebrity arena. You may recall the best-selling purple scarf of last year, well that is a good example of inspiration from a designer range that I just knew would work well. That product created more footfall and adoption of our wider range than any piece has ever done before. It can be small touches that act as tipping points. Have you had any recent wins like that?

Example 4

I: Where do you see yourself five years from now?

C: The world of tourism moves and changes so fast these days that it's difficult to predict too far ahead with any certainty. Do you mind if I share a two-year view?

I: Sure. That would be useful.

C: I have come to love the travel business and in particular travel to Asian countries, so I see myself winning more responsibility and having fun in this region. Recently I helped open the Moscow office for which we won a company award and the Asian portal of our online store has been a key focus of mine over the past two years during which we trebled traffic and quadrupled click-through so online bookings are now best in sector. All of this has enthused me for the region so two years from now I see myself in a role that capitalises on my experience and stretches me even further. Do you see Asia as an important focus for the company's ambitions?

INTERRUPTIONS AND COUNTERPUNCHES

While you are delivering your answers to a question the aggressive interviewer might interrupt and ask for further clarification. These interruptions tend to occur when they sense a perceived weakness or at least weak indicators on your part. Should they find a really sensitive spot they will work it with a series of follow-up questions:

'Sorry. I'm not clear. Why did you say you left ABC Ltd? It sounds like you had a falling out?' Or:

'I'm not sure I really get what role you played in building the sales pipeline. Was this all your own work or did you get some help?'

You mustn't allow an interruption to throw you. Each comeback is a question in its own right. You can use CAP, you can respond with a story:

I: What role did you play in helping the children's charity meet its efficiency objectives?

C: We have made efficiency gains in each of the seven years I have spent with the charity, shall I give you an overview of where we had the most success?

I: Actually I'd like to know if you personally are responsible for the gains or just played a supporting role within a team that drove them?

C: Well, let's take for an example our best year for improvement, which was in 2008 after I had been on board a year. I was responsible for a big-spend budget that the outgoing officer had said needed to be increased. I sat down with the FD to go through the numbers and said I thought I might be able to keep the budget the same or indeed reduce it as I could see it was pretty badly run, so sensed that simple efficiencies should yield a healthy saving. The net of the two key changes I instigated alone netted us just over 30 per cent efficiency gains. I took the plaudits on behalf of my team. How aggressive have you been with efficiency reviews in the past two or three years?

Equally you can meet rapid-fire questions (a common tactic that interviewers like to use to unsettle candidates) with rapid-fire, short responses. Essentially you can counterpunch:

I: What role did you play in the development of the housing estate in Kettering – your CV seems to imply you built it single-handedly!

C: Are you interested in how I execute generally or the Kettering job in particular? I want to be careful when it comes to project specifics not to share anything confidential to ATKIN Partners if that's okay with you.

I: Sure. I respect that. I was looking for as much clarification as you can give me on that job because it is similar to what we do here.

C: I headed the planning and design on Kettering then through the project I provided oversight, so while I didn't place a hand on a single brick I did have a hand in where each was placed.

I: Weren't you just a part of a large planning and design team? What do you mean headed?

C: Yes. At ATKIN Partners we have a matrix model. I was project director for the Kettering job and I nominated the resources I felt we needed to complete the job. As often happens my first- and second-choice team members were for the most part tied up on other commitments so certainly in the early stages I had to weld a team together that were new to me and new to each other. I have to say the team spirit we developed was awesome. We broke a lot of records on that job and I am proud of the industry award we won.

I: So can you work without this estimator and surveyor? Or do we need to poach them too?

C: Sure I can work without them, but I'm always excited by what great people can achieve when they work together. What is the calibre of estimator and surveyor you have on staff today?

It's like a game. You know the rules. You have to ride the punches. Take comfort in the fact that we all have weaknesses and we all know we have weaknesses. This is part of being human. What's important is that you recognise them, learn from them, compensate for them and turn them into strengths.

The interviewer isn't really looking at the weakness itself. This is a sideshow. The interview is an attitude test, because people hire attitude (see page 3). So the genuinely able interviewer is using their question armoury (whatever that might contain) more as a means of testing *how* you respond as opposed to learning more about you because they want to see your attitude.

STEP 8: READY YOUR ANSWERS – KEY POINTS

- Arm yourself with the right attitude, accepting that:
  - No from you is okay.
  - No from the interviewer is okay.
- Use the CAP response framework.
  - Check to make sure you understand the question by ensuring you test your understanding.
  - Ask yourself 'How do I use that question to illustrate my achievements?'
  - Present your answer in an illustrative and compelling way.
- The good interviewer is really looking for your attitude.

STEP 9: NAIL YOUR QUESTIONS

Imagine your interview has just finished. You have left the premises and are heading off. As you reflect on the interview you pat yourself on the back that you have:

1. All the information you need to help you decide whether or not this job is the one for you. You are becoming very clear on this.
2. Convinced the interviewer that you are the ideal candidate for the job or at least that they should endorse you.
3. Agreed the process post-interview and the timing of the next step, or ideally the next series of steps.

What are the questions that led to this outcome? These are what we are going to prepare in this penultimate step.

Everything you need to prepare your interview questions is already in your journal. We are aiming to combine what we have learnt about you in the preceding steps with the wants and needs of the interviewer, to create a persuasive and influential mix. Be in no doubt that the most powerful tool you will use in any interview is the question.

IN THE INTERVIEW YOUR QUESTIONS REIGN SUPREME

At Rembrandt Consultants my team and I have monitored interview feedback from both candidates and interviewers, and the findings provide some interesting insight. In particular, over a two-year period we monitored the ability of both sides to recall certain key aspects that we asked them about. The results make for fascinating reading. As a rough guide, of what the interviewer recalls:

- **80%** of it will be the type, style, content and inflection of your questions
- **15%** the answers that you give
- **5%** other factors

This suggests that you shouldn't spend much time answering questions because the interviewer isn't really taking the information in. Answers *miss*.

It follows that if you want the interviewer to recall something specific then you had better embed it in your questions. Questions *hit*.

A fair question from you at this point would be: 'Hang on a minute. If my questions represent eighty per cent of what the interviewer is going to recall why has this book only got around to preparing them at Step Nine? Surely we should have spent over eighty per cent of the book on this topic?'

Well, in fact, with the exception of Step 6, in which we prepared your stories, all of our other work has been focused on preparing the material that we are going to bring together here to form powerful nail questions. As we know that your questions are what the interviewer remembers, we are going to make sure that your questions have content that will absolutely enable you to nail that interview.

PREPARE, THEN ASK GREAT QUESTIONS

Good questions are at the heart of good selling. I am sure you have heard the sales tip: 'Two ears, one mouth. Use them in that proportion.'

Well, what this sage-like piece of advice fails to do is give you a clue as to how you might do this. It implies simply that you just sit there in silence waiting for your opposite number to speak while you keep an eye on your watch until you have balanced the proportions. Not a good plan.

A better sales tip is: 'Prepare, then ask great questions.' If you ask a good question then the interviewer will answer at some length and indeed they will very likely talk more than you. Which, by the way, is a *very* good thing.

You should be prepared to put a lot of time and energy into this step. Preparing yourself thoroughly now will make the meeting itself a real pleasure for you. You will be free to concentrate on such critical things as the mannerisms and body language of the interviewer. You will be able to control the meeting with more natural ease than you would if you were thinking of questions as you go along.

WHAT DO NAIL QUESTIONS LOOK LIKE?

Nail questions are structured in a format that has been developed over many years by headhunting consultants around the world. While the content and intent of the question will vary, all are structured in the same way:

1. Always open with a clear explanation as to **why** you need the information.
2. Then tell the interviewer something about yourself (**USP**).
3. Finally, ask the **question** (which must relate to real diligence) succinctly and clearly; i.e. you should never have to repeat a question.

So a nail question looks like this:

'It has been important to me to ensure we share manufacturing expertise with the acknowledged experts in Cambridge. I succeeded in improving productivity by more than 30 per cent as a direct result of this sharing model due in large part to being in the community. Tell me, why was the manufacturing plant originally sited in Leeds and would a move in the future be out of the question?'

You can see that when we break this down it fits neatly into the structure outlined above:

- **Why**: It has been important to me to ensure we share manufacturing expertise with the acknowledged experts in Cambridge.
- **USP**: I succeeded in improving productivity by more than 30 per cent as a direct result of this sharing model due in large part to being in the community.
- **Question**: Tell me, why was the manufacturing plant originally sited in Leeds and would a move in the future be out of the question?

Very few candidates write questions out prior to attending interviews and I am really not sure why. It could be ignorance, laziness, lack of time, overconfidence, lack of confidence or perhaps a combination of one or more of these I guess. There is nothing stopping you from preparing well-structured and detailed questions in advance and taking them into the interview with you.

Having learnt to nail interviews you will be in a different league entirely to these ill-prepared candidates as you *will* be taking your prepared questions in with you. Furthermore, since we know that 80 per cent of the interviewer's recollection is going to be your questions, you will put in the extra effort required to turn them into nail questions that will open doors to career opportunities.

DIFFERENCE BETWEEN WEAK AND STRONG QUESTIONS

To further illustrate the value of good question structure, let's consider a weak question for a moment:

'Why do you only provide the free book and DVD service for the elderly in the North East region?'

Ouch! It is unlikely that the answer to this question is going to move the interviewer forwards positively in their view of you as a candidate, so this type of throwaway question, while okay, makes you look like the average job hunter who couldn't think of anything more intelligent to ask. While it is succinct, this question fails to clarify:

- Why do you need this information?
- What does this question tell the interviewer about you?

It is a wasted question. None of your questions can be one-liners. With this sort of question there is a very real risk that the interviewer, who isn't absolutely clear as to what information is needed here, will trail off on any number of tangents with their answer and use up lots of valuable time. This is time that neither the candidate nor they can afford to waste.

So structure is fundamental to get the information *you* need and to ensure the interviewer gets what *they* need.

A stronger question would look something like this:

'I know from the work I have been doing in the Midlands and the South that the elderly feel more valued by their local community and indeed more in touch with them when they are able to share experiences of contemporary media. Similarly all our recent test findings suggest that door knocking for gifts of books and DVDs is proving more successful than asking for cash.

'Tell me why confine the free book and DVD service for the elderly to the North East region and would a move to develop it nationwide be looked on favourably?'

This clearly fits the nail question structure. It is certainly well articulated, challenging and informed.

Imagine for a moment that you're the interviewer. Can you imagine being on the receiving end of this style of question? Your thoughts would probably be along the lines of:

1. I get the sense that this candidate is carrying out genuine diligence on the way we as a management team make important decisions about where to invest our time and money – if I don't cover this question well they might not want to join. I had better start to sell.
2. I certainly think he understands the importance of why the elderly people we care for value one of our key initiatives

here in the North East and he has a track record testing his ideas with real field research – that is something we need. I like this trait particularly since many of our good initiatives have been allowed to die on the vine while some of our worst are pressed through on one daft political agenda or another!

Questions framed in the right way and with the correct content drawn from your research will tell the interviewer that you understand their business and can empathise with many of the issues they need to manage day to day.

EXAMPLES OF STRONG QUESTIONS

Here are some example questions with the structure clearly labelled to help you gain a better grasp of what a well-formed question looks like. You will be aiming to ask questions throughout the meeting. As opposed to seeing the meeting as being a game of two halves (first half the interviewer questions you; the second half you question the interviewer), see it as a free-flowing conversation into which you can weave your questions as you see and feel best at the time. Despite the fact that we are focusing in this step specifically on developing your questions, don't get the impression that your nail questions are asked one after the other in a predetermined order.

Remember that one of the key objectives you are aiming to nail here is to answer the question 'Do I want the job?' Your questions of the interviewer should therefore be phrased to ensure that you yield the information you need about the role to help you answer this. Do bear in mind as you work on your questions that while interviewing for a specific job what you are really asking yourself is this: 'What has to happen for the job I am interviewing for to serve as a sturdy rung in the stepladder to my dream career?' Bear this in mind when you read through these examples. If you need to remind yourself of the structure, take a look back at page 131.

Value-biased questions that help ensure the opportunity fits well in your personal career frame:

- **Why**: I am really interested in the spirit and atmosphere within the business and how it can positively affect performance.
- **USP**: At EXCO I helped change the spirit for the better as leader of the sports and social club. We really gelled with one another outside work. Even those who didn't play enthusiastically came to watch and support. The positive spirit helped us yield a higher performance threshold from the team – we soon left old records way behind.
- **Question**: What sort of initiatives do you run today to help inspire the troops to greater heights?
- **Why**: I have this burning desire to give back, to help others less fortunate than I am.
- **USP**: In EXCO I have agreed a simple deal with my manager whereby once I have exceeded my targets by 10 per cent for the month I get one day to spend with the local kids' hospice doing some voluntary work.
- **Question**: Do you have anything similar in place? How best do you think we could make this work?'

A skills/technical-biased question that checks the role is suited to your skills, experience and approach:

- **Why**: I read the quarterly update comment that the business is going through a tough period with sales cycles getting longer as indecision and uncertainty bites.
- **USP**: At EXCO I spent time and extra care ensuring that whenever possible we requalified all threats to the cycle with our clients so we identified all of the problem cycles and put extra incentives on the table to keep the spotlight on them and do whatever was necessary to keep them at full momentum. We managed to shorten most of the cycles and indeed pull out of cycles that we identified as not responding, so probably ineffective anyway.

- **Question**: How much responsibility do you give to sales for qualification and how would you rate the team at this right now?

YOUR NAIL QUESTIONS

Can you begin to imagine what your nail questions need to look like? You need to prepare 20 questions. Not because you will use all 20 in a single interview but because:

1. You are preparing yourself to carry out diligence on your future career platform and you are entering a process that simply begins with this interview. In the subsequent stages you will have the opportunity to take your diligence further. Get ready now.
2. You must never run out of questions.
3. The process of prioritising your questions will ensure you enter the first interview with the cream of the crop. Your top 10 questions!

Have a go at formulating a question or two of your own. Bear in mind that you cannot ask questions about information obviously available in the public domain. You need to dig deeper than that. There aren't any rules on the process to build these questions, just very clear guidelines on how they should look when they are finished. However, below I've suggested a process that may help you start to form your questions.

1. Try choosing one of your USPs from Step 5 (see pages 70–73) and write it in the middle of a new page of your journal.
2. Now pick a value that is important to you from those you identified in Step 2 (see page 35). Note it at the top of the page.

3. Then turn to your research on the role (see Step 7, pages 81–112) and select a related aspect that you need further clarity on. Write this down at the bottom of the page.

Having written these three notes you simply fill in the gaps, keeping the USP at the heart, to form a question. Don't be too particular about the precise wording at this stage. I am more concerned that you become comfortable with the structure for now. Here's an example:

- **Why**: Honesty – a straight talker, I tend to like people to be straight with me.
- **USP**: I have worked on book projects across very diverse genres, from lifestyle to sport and fiction to autobiography.
- **Question**: How do you maintain high design standards as cost pressures continue to grow?

Then fill in the gaps to form a question as follows:

'I like straight and direct conversation, not beating around the bush, so I'd like to get your views on managing the cost pressures that we know continue to grow. I have worked on book projects across very diverse genres from lifestyle to sport and fiction to autobiography, which seems to have made me a popular choice with commissioners who appreciate my flexibility and efficiency. Tell me how do you and your team go about maintaining high design standards despite ever increasing cost pressure?'

Once you have this first question down in draft form pat yourself on the back – you have your first nail question! Try saying this question out loud. I know you will need to polish it a little (or a lot!), but recognise that you are now preparing questions that are truly at the nail it end of very good.

You can begin to see now that, provided you use high-quality information, this simple question model powerfully nails your two primary objectives:

1. **Do you want the job?** Provided you are clear on the gaps you have in your understanding then your questions will draw clear answers to give you complete clarity and ensure you are equipped to answer this, your headline objective.

2. **Persuade the interviewer to want you for the job.** Because you have Objective 1 as your priority you will come across as a discerning careerist who is very clear and determined to get what you want. This is very noticeable to the interviewer. Your USPs will be powerfully embedded in the interviewer's head. They have to listen to them carefully because this is a question and you are going to want an answer. Your current and succinct questions will genuinely challenge the interviewer.

Now try and build a question back to front, by beginning with the succinct question at the end. Make sure it is genuinely a question you seek the answer to and something you really are interested to know about. Ideally the question should be about a subject that you know will be somewhat challenging for the interviewer. You will soon find that formulating questions in this structure will become very familiar and you will rattle them off.

20 QUESTIONS

Keep going with formulating your questions. Be as strict as you can with the structure. Try to draw on elements from your journal as you go. Make every question a nail question.

When you have 10 questions written down take a break. Put your journal away and come back to it 24 hours later. Reread the questions and give them a polish.

Now press on and see if you can get 10 more down. This may require a cold flannel to your forehead as you press your brain to the limits; however, better to experience the discomfort now than when sat in front of an interviewer.

Once you've got your next 10 questions down, again, put your journal to one side. Let your mind rest and it will usually come back with inspired gusto to provide you with good self-critique a day later.

Now carefully select your top 10 questions from the list. It might be that you prefer to blend two okay questions together to form one great one – that is fine.

PROMPT SHEET #2

Type up your top 10 questions using the nail question structure. Here's an example:

1	Why	It has been important to me to ensure we share manufacturing expertise with the acknowledged experts in Cambridge.
	USP	I succeeded in improving productivity by more than 30 per cent as a direct result of this sharing model due in large part to being IN the community.
	Question	Tell me why was the manufacturing plant originally sited in Leeds and would a move in the future be out of the question?

Type up your other nine questions in the same way. Leave a space for a Question 11: we'll come on to this in a moment. Print a copy off. This is your first draft of Prompt Sheet #2 that you will take with you into the interview (see page 146).

YOUR VISION QUESTION

Look over Prompt Sheet #2. You now need to come up with your Question 11 – this is what I refer to as the vision question.

In essence the vision question should ask:

What has to happen for this job to act as a foothold for my climb to the summit I aspire to conquer?

Your vision question is the sharp and visible tip of your assured self. Your career is your concern and you do not intend to mess around when there is a clear opportunity to cut to the chase with someone who can support your progress or even accelerate it.

In the vision question are captured sentiments that will polarise opinion among the interviewing purists. The question can be seen as aggressive, pushy and overzealous. It might even be construed as a little rude since it apparently presents the entry role as simply a stepping stone to be used momentarily on your way to a far more meaningful ambition.

Once you have asked it you can grant yourself entry into the exclusive *Nail That Interview* club because you will truly have graduated from the ranks of those who simply attend job interviews to the elite few who use interviews to help navigate their career trajectory for optimum progress.

Ask yourself the questions:

What do I ultimately want to know from the interviewer I am about to meet?

What can they really do for my career if they are so minded?

Phrasing your vision question into something you are comfortable with that is also relevant to the situation and the person you are meeting with is worth spending a little time on, but do keep it simple and focused. The question in simple form looks like:

Can this become a good step for my career? What has to happen for this to become a great *step for my career?*

When you wear your heart on your sleeve you feel liberated. Those whom you meet will feel comfortable dropping the barriers that usually exist between people in professional meetings.

Placed within the nail format you might phrase your question like this:

11	Why	My vision one day is to be head of marketing for an aspirational midsize business like this.
	USP	I love what I do and for me work is very important – I eat, sleep and breathe it. I have always worked hard to identify the skills and experience gaps I have and then fill them with the best training and exposure I can find. Luckily I have been privileged to work with exceptional people who have willingly helped me climb the tall career ladder.
	Question	If we project forwards in time and I have done an outstanding job for you in this role, how do you feel my career could best plot a route to a head of marketing level?

Use the vision question wisely. It's a powerful tool; one that needs to be respected. The benefit of Question 11 is that it serves to reveal what might lie beyond the job that is the immediate subject of the interview to probe the possibilities at the extremities over time. This is the invitation to the interviewer to put their brains into gear for you personally and imagine what might be for *you*.

EXAMPLES OF VISION QUESTIONS

11	Why	For this, my first real career footing out of education, I would like to join a business that has the capacity to found great careers from entry through to retirement.
	USP	While most of those around me have stepped in and out of courses, societies and commitments, I have always stuck rigidly to seeing things through no matter what and I think that has yielded some of my greatest achievements and indeed fun that they have missed. I am a committed and loyal person to my core so it is really important I choose the first step well.
	Question	Are there any examples of people in senior positions who worked their way up the ladder that we could share as role models?

11	Why	I was fortunate to have the opportunity to work my way around the world in my gap year.
	USP	The world feels small and yet massive. The possibilities that exist for businesses to take proven initiatives and franchise them to a global audience I find really exciting. I have sold more to Far Eastern clients on my eBay store than in the UK!
	Question	Given your global reach, how much travel do you expect an internal audit clerk would do in a typical year?

11	Why	I'd like to stretch my legs beyond the design office and gain more exposure to clients.
	USP	I have been directly involved in the concept phase of three of the five award-winning concepts our firm has produced this year. I understand that with just three years in this role I need to serve time but I feel I have far more to offer by helping clients be brave. I won art scholarships using digital media that is still used on the school's website today – I had to persuade them of the concept and apply for the funding to build it. Believe me, school governors are a tough sell when they have no budget!
	Question	What opportunities do you think this role offers me to work directly with clients and how soon might that develop?

THE MOST IMPORTANT QUESTION?

The vision question has to be asked at the right time. By this stage your interviewer should have been persuaded to want you for the job or at least be inclined in this direction. With the vision question you are cheekily adding the final blows of the hammer while also exploring the career potential that this role and this company might offer you.

In the rare and privileged moments that follow your having asked your vision question you get a glimpse of your destiny (or at least what it could be).

*

What is revealed about the interviewer is critical:

- **Weak boss**: Your interviewer might choose to react negatively and put you in your place, emphasising that you should not presume to dream, rather you should do as you are told and stay in your place.
- **Bad dream**: They might paint you a scenario or two that, however hard you try, you fail to be inspired by; career routes and loops that you just can't buy.
- **Good dream**: On the other hand, perhaps they describe a career loop that you find hugely inspiring; one littered with opportunity and choice in which you just feel sure you cannot fail to reach the vision you aspire to and have fun along the way.
- **Good boss**: Ideally your empathetic interviewer is prompted to put in the effort necessary to help you find the route to your vision from this opening foothold. They want you to join them, to accept the job and they value that you are serious about progressing towards your dream. They get excited by what you can do *together*.

So, the vision question is an important question. Perhaps *the* most important question of your set. The use of this question can help develop a strong bond between you and the hiring authority, who should want to be associated with bringing in great people.

Phrase this question in a way that feels natural for you and add it to your list of nail questions to complete Prompt Sheet #2.

STEP 9: NAIL YOUR QUESTIONS – KEY POINTS

- Questions reign supreme; 80 per cent of what the interviewer will recall will be the type, style, content and inflection of your questions.
- Nail your questions:
  1. Always open with a clear explanation as to why you need the information.
  2. Then tell the interviewer something about yourself (USP).
  3. Ask the question (which must relate to real diligence) succinctly and clearly.
- Choose your top 10 nail questions.
- Add Question 11, your vision question, to Prompt Sheet #2. This question differs from your top 10 questions as it invites the interviewer to join you on a journey to your vision. The answer to this question provides insight into the interviewer, the company and the future possibilities that you only get the opportunity to see:
  1. in the interview meeting
  2. by asking Question 11 – your final blow of the hammer!
- You only have 60 minutes and it's your career at stake, so prepare, then ask great questions.

STEP 10: PRACTICE

So, you have completed nine steps. In this final step you are going to use all the work you've done so far and practise being in an interview situation. It is the final attention to detail in this step that can be critical when it comes to ensuring the ultimate sale of you (the product), ensuring that you really do nail it.

Before you start practising, there is one other task that you need to do. You are going to assemble your *interview pack*. One of the questions candidates most frequently ask me is 'What do I actually take into the interview with me?' The answer is, you take your interview pack. And I'm going to tell you exactly what you need to put in it and how to use it. You will need it when you're practising.

WHY PRACTISE?

I am sure you sense the need for practice that will let you test all that you have prepared so far – to hone the questions and the stories and explore how best you can present the points that you want to make.

Rehearsal and practice are an essential part of any good performance. All of our achievements are built on the experience and insight that a series of prior attempts afford us. Some of those attempts might have been close, others miserable failures. In the end we are successful because we learn from failure.

First, then, accept that you need to fail. In order to truly nail interviews you must first fail in a safe place *before* the interview itself.

Practice is the safe environment within which failure is welcomed, enjoyed and laughed at. Actors have a great laugh in rehearsals – an acknowledged part of delivering a good performance on the night is that they explore and find enjoyment in the role during the rehearsal phase. You too should enjoy your practice. Refine and learn your lines. Find the fun. Laugh at your own expense.

INTERVIEW PACK

Your pack contains:

- Two clean copies of your CV (see Step 1)
- Prompt Sheet #1 – your stories (see Step 6)
- Prompt Sheet #2 – your nail questions (see Step 9)

Interviewers, in my experience, are always impressed with candidates who are well prepared. In fact they usually remark on this, with a comment such as 'I am glad to see you have prepared so thoroughly'.

I have never had an interviewer come back to me to say that they felt a candidate was over-prepared. So please be assured that you should have your interview pack with you and you should feel free to pull out its contents, when you feel it is appropriate to do so, to show the interviewer that as far as you are concerned this is *your* meeting and you are going to get from it what *you* need to make it a success for *you*.

WORKING FROM THE SAME PAGE

Do make sure that the CV you have with you at the interview is the same version that the interviewer has if you have already sent it to them.

PRACTICE SCHEDULE

I have drafted an ideal practice schedule for you and assumed you have four days for final preparation, which would be ideal. If you have less you will have to condense your practice, more would be a welcome luxury. Regardless of how much time you actually have available be fair to yourself – you have put a lot of effort into taking each of the nine steps and completing your interview pack, so please don't bypass Step 10 entirely. Using the techniques and exercises in this step can really be the difference between okay and exceptional, between amateur and professional.

Taking four days to prepare, I recommend you split the time into two equal phases that help you build up slowly:

Phase 1: Two days – Visualisation and self-appraisal
1½ hours per day x 2 = 3 hours
Phase 2: Two days – Role play
1½ hours per day x 2 = 3 hours

Total – 6 hours

Working through this two-phase schedule over a four-day period will help ensure that you feel completely familiar with the interview experience when the time comes that you interview for real.

We have found these phases work because they provide you with an insight into where you are comfortable and strong, and indeed what your weaknesses are and what you need to take another look at. Your early experiments with visualisation set your mind to work on refining the message and delivery, helping you practise and work on presentation using a variety of different approaches.

PHASE 1: TWO DAYS – VISUALISATION AND SELF-APPRAISAL

For each of your first two practice days book a 1½-hour slot in your diary, preferably at the end of the day. Arrange it so that you can be in a quiet and private space where you won't be disturbed. If you have more than four days before your interview, by all means spread this phase out, the days don't need to be back to back.

Just as students are encouraged to sit mock exams, I am going to take you through a couple of visualised interview dry runs to help prepare you for the interview proper. Indeed, by the time you are actually sitting face to face with your interviewer I would like you to have done the meeting several times over in your mind so that you are as well prepared mentally as you can be.

Because visualisation is just a simulation we can measure and monitor several aspects of your performance that will help you gauge your performance better on the big day. The first aspect I would like to focus on is timing.

TIMING

It is important that you are aware of how long certain aspects of the discussion take so make sure you have a stopwatch or a clock (preferably digital) in view. You will own responsibility for managing time on the day and despite us all being sure we know how long a minute is, most people don't get it right when tested. You need to get a good feel for how long you are taking to ask questions and deliver answers. If you don't manage to ask one or other of your stronger questions or perhaps have to hurry your best story then you will have to accept the blame.

Here's how the timings of an ideal interview break down:

Timing cues and clues		
	Number delivered	Total minutes
Greetings and welcome	1	3
Candidate's selected questions	6	6
Candidate's stories	2	5
Candidate's answers	6	12
Candidate's Question 11	1	1

Interviewer questions	6	6
Interviewer answers	7	21
Closing remarks	1	4
Farewell	1	2
TOTAL		60

In this balanced meeting the ratios are nicely evened up. Both the candidate and the interviewer get to ask six questions each (plus the candidate asks their Question 11). Actually, this is quite a lot more than we typically see fitted into a one-hour meeting, but let's begin with ideals and work from there.

For this example meeting to work most effectively for you, you can see that you have to keep your answers to just two minutes, while we have allowed the interviewer three. I would encourage you to try to maintain and hold this proportion as the ideal.

Of course, you cannot control what the interviewer does. How long they speak for is up to them, but you do influence how much they have to say through the quality of your questions and your preparedness to allow them the space to answer – only interrupting them where time constraints compel you to do so.

You will also note that I have allowed both the candidate and the interviewer a minute for each question that they both want to ask. This will include the clarifiers that both use (you will be using your CAP technique, see page 115).

Of course, in the real world interviews run in different ways or for different lengths of time. Some run for two hours or more, some just thirty minutes. Some interviewers like to talk – and talk! I have a client who usually manages to answer just two questions before the interview time is up as he is a huge gasbag. So, the table above is a good guide as to the pace you should aim for in your meeting.

WALK-THROUGH

To get things rolling I think it best that I actually walk you into an interview meeting. If you have never attended a serious job interview before this will help set the scene. Even if you have some or a lot of experience with interviews I think you will find this helps get you in the right mood to practise.

To bring this walk-through to life I'd like you to imagine you are a fly on the wall of a real-life interview. You see the candidate enter the building, smell the fresh paint or perhaps polish in the office and listen to the pleasant greeting the receptionist gives the candidate as they announce themselves. They sign the visitors' book, then sit down to wait in reception. A few minutes pass before they are invited to go through at the allotted time.

🕐   Start the stopwatch (or make a note of the time on your watch). The meeting has begun.

The interviewer greets them.

They shake hands and smile. We can predict the line of conversation at this stage with reasonable confidence because this type of comfortable small talk is almost universal across the human race:

1. *How are you?*
2. *Have you come far?*
3. *Is this a part of the town/region/country you know well?*
4. *Coffee or tea? Milk, sugar?*

I call them 'settler questions'. They help both parties ease into the meeting proper and provide some welcome normality to what is otherwise a first experience for both parties (i.e. they haven't met before!).

Here is what I have encouraged the candidate you are watching to do at this point of the meeting:

Slow down! There is an opportunity at the beginning of every interview to help settle things down and by doing so help the interviewer to get comfortable with you quickly. I have to be honest here and say that it's not that easy; however, you really can visualise this in action.

See the candidate use these settler questions; see them delivering the answers simply, clearly and calmly.

They are *really* calm.

Subconsciously they try to make the meeting slow down and relax. Think 'We have all the time in the world'. Notice how they maintain eye contact when it feels natural to do so.

Slow down!	*I am very well, thank you. And you?*
Slow down!	*It took me thirty-five minutes, things are working today, thanks.*
Slow down!	*I have passed through the area several times but I haven't really explored – do you think I should?*
Slow down!	*Coffee for me please. Milk without. Thank you.*

By calmly helping to set the pace and tempo of the meeting they are sending an important message to the interviewer that they are comfortable sharing control with them. They will help to make this meeting a success for both interviewer and candidate. For the purposes of the visualisation it is worth thinking about the interviewer pitching (or bowling if you prefer cricket) a ball at the candidate in the form of questions, challenges and tests.

First ball from the interviewer:

Look at the candidate sat opposite the interviewer. You can see their coffee in front of them. They take a sip. They haven't placed the prompt sheets I helped them prepare in front of them just yet, but they are close to hand in the folder by their chair. Take note of how the interviewer looks. Take note of the room and their surroundings. Take note of the smells.

Your faculty for visualisation is immense. You can run this whole interview in your mind in an infinite number of ways and with endless variables, so have a little of fun.

Check the time – greetings and welcome – three minutes elapsed?

The interviewer asks the classic opener that we began Step 1 with:

> I: *Thank you for coming along this afternoon. Would you mind beginning with a little bit about yourself? Just take me through the highlights. You know, tell me who you are.*
> C: *Sure.*

Our candidate responds calmly recalling their CAP (see page 115):

> C: *Can I just check that you have a copy of my CV?*

As they say this they reach calmly into their folder and pull out their CV along with their prompt sheets. They place them on the desk.

> C: *Any particular aspect of my career or more particularly my recent achievements you would like me to focus on?*
> I: *Yes, I have your CV. Please just take me through the highlights if you would.*
> C: *Sure. I got into fashion by accident or should I say luck? The college I was accepted for didn't have enough applicants to fill the home economics course I was booked on to but they happened to have spaces left for fashion and textiles, which is a subject I had enjoyed but not really engaged with at that time, so as opposed to moving college I opted in and I loved it from the moment I got my hands on the mannequin in the garment studio. I was hooked and …*

And they are away. They keep it brief, highlighting their strong points. They courteously use the question to deliver some of the important features and achievements that they want to mention from their FAB (see pages 71–74), albeit they will cover them again.

(🕐)   Candidate answers – two minutes per answer?

Then they round out by asking a well-framed question that balances the control of the meeting:

(ⓨ)　Candidate asks question – one minute including clarifier?

Imagine them calmly delivering a question here that they have selected from their Prompt Sheet #2.

Second ball from the interviewer:
> I: *Why do you want to work here? What is it that draws you to our company at this time?*

Candidate pauses and thinks CAP.

This sort of question is very open in style – they can answer this in a variety of ways and styles, for example they could use one of the stories from their Prompt Sheet #1. Consider how they might get from this question to their story. How might the link be smoothly made?

Or they might pick out one or two of the more particular traits they have learnt in their research (Step 7) and impress the interviewer with their understanding.

If you can't see clearly how they might handle this question then go back to Step 8 and refresh yourself on the attitude you should wear and the way you apply CAP. The CAP can be used as well here as with any question. Here the candidate keeps the answer very short and moves to one of the key lines of questioning that they want to pursue.

> C: *I am enjoying what I do immensely, but I feel the need to explore what I am really capable of and there are pretty clear lines of constraint in my current role. I understand from Polly, who introduced us, that here at Miss Only there is more opportunity to spread your wings. How do you manage to keep control of overall product design while allowing each team member such high levels of freedom?*

(ⓨ)　Candidate has up to two minutes per answer so no need to rush it.

Third ball from the interviewer:

I: *When things have gone wrong in an account one of your team is leading, how do you decide when to parachute in and take charge?*

Candidate pauses, thinks CAP and then responds:

C: *It depends on what's gone wrong. How serious. But I think you're looking more at the trust and empowerment I confer and how that actually works in reality, is that more the angle?*

I: *Yes. Precisely how do you behave with them when it seems all is not as it should be?*

The thinking time has allowed the candidate to look over their stories on Prompt Sheet #1 and consider a link to one that looks relevant. They deliver it calmly:

C: *Trust is built and earned over time. You get to know the team members as individuals and while the process framework helps with general direction and standards I try to make sure it doesn't stifle individual flair. I prefer to nourish and encourage that flair as I find it boosts performance mostly.*
(Story 1) There is a woman on my team who I plucked from another region. She is a really ambitious person and it has always been a challenge holding back her ambitions to allow her true capability to keep pace in case she stumbled, or worse, fell. She was adamant that we were going to win the opportunity to put a concession in John Lewis. In our regular team meeting she mentioned that John Lewis had asked Astral to submit a bid for this concession also, just for good governance. I saw this as an ideal opportunity to help insure her position without offending her. Astral are a company we really need to know a little more about. Let's use this as an opportunity to get a bit more on them. Please can you involve Roger to double-check precisely where we are and how they intend to measure us versus Astral to make their decision? We need all we can get on these guys and anything we can do to ensure our winning of this should be done.'

Roger found a lot of holes, which once plugged, with her help, did win us this key concession. In Roger's view, however, we were at best fifty-fifty to win what it transpired was a concession that turned into the foundation stone for several years of really profitable brand placement. We can't say for sure that we wouldn't have won it without him, but in hindsight I shudder that my inclination to intervene carefully and in a complementary way had apparently been so important.

The quality of the people in the team is key. I like to get involved as a leader wherever and whenever I feel insurance is required. I try to do this in a way that complements the team. I won't do the job for them. How would you rate the team members in place at the moment?

Candidate's stories – two and a half minutes? Should be well within this time during visualisation; however, it's amazing how the time flies by in the actual interview.

I: *Are you still hands-on personally with your own accounts?*

C: *Absolutely, but just the one. Even with this one major account I am planning to begin to give my assistants more responsibility. I'm aiming to make them less dependent on me over the next six months or so.*

(Story 2) When I originally won the Juniper account it sprang from a fashion show I had helped design for in New York for the autumn launch of the teen range. The head of buying had caught me after the show. She was under huge pressure and I think in fear for her job. Right there in the conference hall we sat down for a coffee and had a really frank conversation about the marketplace and how samey it had all become. She had really been drawn to a few of the peculiarities of the range I had helped pull together at quite short notice. I explained where I got the inspiration from and how I had wanted to be bolder but had been held back by the large layer of interfering bureaucrats who sat above me at the time. She really needed my help and she asked 'When can you start?' We have been working together for over

six years now. The act of delegating comes easily to me but I have appreciated the opportunity to keep Juniper as my opportunity to stay connected to the front line. I would prefer to retain a bit of hands-on throughout my career from here. How does the split look among your other designers?

🕐 Read it out loud. Two and a half minutes to deliver?

Fourth ball from the interviewer:

I: *Do you have any further questions for me?*

Actually I wouldn't expect the candidate to be asked this question as they have been weaving questions into the meeting from the beginning. However, if we imagine the question being used in this walk-through it will serve well as an indicator of the way control might be gifted to the candidate to see what they will do with it. This may be an indication that the interviewer has covered the obvious questions they have and they want some direction from the candidate. After all, if the candidate is steering the meeting the interviewer can sit back a little and assess the candidate from a different angle.

C: *Yes. I've made a note of my questions and it would be good to cover some of them here today, so can I begin with one that I'm sure you will be expecting?*

The shift to online as part of omni-channel is accelerating globally and the reach of the client through technology into the business is something we are still only beginning to explore. At Juniper I set up a focus group to look at whether women were interested in being able to plug and play with costumes and accessories to create complete looks on screen and we had what can only be described as huge enthusiasm for the notion. How dynamic do you feel you are here at taking this sort of early enthusiasm and turning it into online solutions that really deliver on the promise?

🕐 Read it out loud. How long to deliver?

By all means continue the interview as you play fly-on-the wall. Keep an eye on the clock and draw it to a close at the hour mark.

I hope you can begin to see how as you practise you should aim to press yourself with the more challenging questions. This is something you are actually likely to be rather good at now having completed the 10 steps.

Reread all or part of the walk-through and imagine yourself taking long pauses then responding with a clarification question followed by a series of clear and clipped answers. Embrace pauses. They can help you control the pace of the meeting.

Your assuredness can't help but impress the interviewer, who will likely cede control of the meeting allowing you to use one or more of your well-prepared questions.

WORK ON YOUR QUESTIONS AND STORIES

From your interview pack pull out your prompt sheets. Try some of your questions out for size. Read them aloud and time yourself as you do so.

Do they feel a little long-winded or over-elaborate? Have a go at making them more punchy. Use a highlighter pen to pick out the central themes so you don't have to read them word for word.

Imagine that you have an interviewer sat in front of you and they are asking you questions. Put them on the clock as they phrase their question or preamble (remember that interviewers are likely to be only loosely prepared for the interview so will often talk about a semi-relevant point for two or three times longer than they ought to so let the clock run a little as you imagine them waffling on).

Keep rewinding to a particularly interesting or challenging question and each time deliver a different response. If it feels a little whacky or if you lose your train of thought then laugh at yourself (don't get critical or negative), rewind and run it again. This is your early read-through, your rehearsal. You will learn more from your mistakes and slip-ups than you do from smooth delivery.

By all means press the pause button and have a break. Just pick up where you left off. Stop when you have spent an hour and a half visualising yourself either answering questions or asking them – and even a mixture of both. Don't worry if there are questions you feel you didn't quite nail in this session. Your brain will continue to play with all of the material ahead of your next rehearsal.

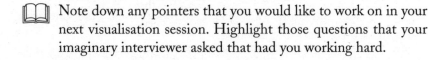 Check over the times you took for each question and answer, note them in your journal and compare the results with the Timing cues and clues table on pages 148–149.

Note down any pointers that you would like to work on in your next visualisation session. Highlight those questions that your imaginary interviewer asked that had you working hard.

All of this is training your brain, developing your subconscious ability through imagined, yet realistic experience to better equip you for the interview. It will help to make you more familiar with how and when the prompt-sheet content can best be used and woven into the interview dialogue.

YOUR INTERVIEW VISUALISATION

Now run your own visualisation of the interview meeting. Take it from the top. Aim to run the meeting right the way through.

Sit comfortably, but sit upright (don't lie down or you may find yourself asleep). Close your eyes. Relax your body. Clear the clutter from your mind (use whatever technique works for you; I like to use the meditation technique of imagining a burning candle).

Imagine yourself arriving at the interview. Feel the stirring of butterflies in your tummy as those healthy nerves get to work (see box).

I recommend you fast-forward through scene setting to focus more time on the challenging and testing elements of the meeting. By now you should be starting to enjoy a feeling of familiarity with the interview and this is precisely what we are aiming to develop.

Keep an eye on the clock as you work through the various stages. You should begin to get a feel for how the seconds pass and the minutes disappear – the precious time needs managing carefully. Are you getting your questions and answers delivered succinctly and powerfully?

BUTTERFLY FORMATION

The body's nervous system has become finely tuned through millions of years of evolution to be alert to danger and threats of any kind. It is quite natural for you to feel the system kick into action whenever you place yourself outside of your routine and comfort zone and whenever you expose yourself to stress of any kind.

The interview is one of those meetings that will benefit from your being more alert as a result of this nervous kick. Welcome the feeling.

Toastmasters International (a non-profit educational organisation that teaches public speaking and leadership skills) has a sage piece of advice for aspiring public speakers: 'Get your butterflies flying in formation.' By which they mean line your nerves up to work positively on your delivery. This advice applies equally to the interview scenario.

Use your nerves to sharpen your wit and wake you up like a caffeine shot. The day you aren't nervous going into an interview should be the day you retire!

Nerves are good!

THE 'I LIKE YOU' TRICK

Add a simple yet powerful sales trick into your visualisation that really does work when meeting people for the first time.

As you imagine yourself looking at your interviewer who is asking you a question or perhaps answering one of your questions, simply say to yourself 'I really do like you!' As you say this feel like you really mean it.

Note how differently you pose your questions, how you alter your seating posture, how your face lights up as you lean in towards them. Your subconscious body language transmits a powerful message of 'I like you!'

People like people who like them.

Note down all of the key questions your interviewer asked you in your visualisation. This will act as the script for your partner or friend in the role play to come.

PHASE 2: TWO DAYS – ROLE PLAY

You have come as far as you reasonably can on your own. Now you need to find a willing accomplice to help you elevate your rehearsal to a more realistic level. It really doesn't matter who you use but I would suggest that ideally:

1. They are game for a laugh. This needs to be fun. Just like the rehearsing actors I mentioned earlier, you will gain far more from your practice if you are prepared to laugh at yourself.
2. They have an intellect broadly similar or ideally slightly above your own.
3. They have professional experience of interviews themselves as a reference point. If they don't have this they will be less inclined to play the role of interviewer convincingly.

SCENE SETTING

Play one or more of the classic power games that interviewers play:

- Have the interviewer sit behind a big desk.
- Place the interviewer on a tall chair while you sit looking up at them from a small one.
- Have the interviewer's back to a wall and yours to a window or door.

All of these will give the interviewer an added sense of authority and superiority over you. The more games like this you play the better you will get. Work on giving yourself a hard time in this safe setting.

You will need two sessions with your 'interviewer' of an hour and a half each. Find a room or space that you can practise in that feels like an appropriate mock interview room.

Help your friend to step into their role as interviewer by:

1. Sharing the company and role specification you are being interviewed for.
2. Outlining the background to the interviewer that they will be impersonating.
3. Running through your CV. As you do so use a highlighter pen to pick out areas where you would expect the interviewer to focus their attention and explain what they might seek.
4. Providing a list of questions – make them the toughest you can think up.
5. Ask them to have fun but to try and give you a hard time. Can they keep a poker face and grill you to make you squirm?

YOUR INTERVIEW REHEARSAL

There are all sorts of tricks you can try that might help add realism and get you both into the right spirit, but simply beginning with a knock on the door and the sharing of pleasantries combined with the pouring of a cup of tea or coffee should be a good start.

(Ⓨ) Make sure you time the meeting.

Kick off the interview and just keep going. Your interviewer is an impersonator so of course they are going to go off on a few weird tangents. Help them back with your questions and answers. Try to stay in character and encourage your interviewer to do the same.

If the wheels come off and you both curl up in balls of laughter – fantastic. There is no better tonic for your rehearsal. It is probable that, through humour, you will gain greater insight into the meeting's possibilities than you ever would without the giggles. Having laughed yourselves out, get back on track until your next fit hits you!

As in theatre rehearsals, and all rehearsal drills for that matter, the experience of rehearsing is often cited as being a lot more difficult than the real thing. This is obviously good, so welcome it.

At 60 minutes, prompt, declare the meeting closed.

FEEDBACK

Ask for critique. Welcome their initial reactions. Don't prompt them to start with, simply ask them how they feel you did. These early reflections are important. If necessary, encourage them to be harsh. You need honest responses. Press them to pick out the little details.

Write their key points down. Don't get into a discussion yet. You should find that the act of writing as they speak encourages them to articulate their thoughts more fully. You are showing them great respect by visibly demonstrating the value you attach to their impression of you and your performance. You are also, by the way, setting them up for the second performance, which you should have scheduled for the following day or not long thereafter. 'Crikey, if they pay this much attention to what I think about their interview performance I had better pay attention to the detail tomorrow!'

When your friend is all talked out you have two final questions for them:

1. Can you recall the main features and benefits that make me a shoo-in for this role?

What we are hopefully going to see here is that they have listened to your nail questions in particular and that the contents have sunk in. This should be quite an amusing little test of memory recall. Note down how they did.

2. Will you offer me the job?

Or how about 'close for next steps'? This is the business end of the interview meeting and where the final objective is played out. Essentially you are looking to get your friend's thoughts as to your appropriateness for the role and how well that came across. Of course it is difficult for them to be completely objective because they aren't actually the hiring authority but they should be pretty good at pretending. As opposed to asking 'Will you offer me the job?', this is a good time to try out a few closing lines. We find many of our candidates are wary of pressing for clarity at the end of the interview, but as with any business or professional meeting it is good practice to clarify the current situation and what comes next. There are an infinite number of ways of asking for this clarity and you should find an approach you are comfortable with and practise it here. How about these for instance:

> *'I have plenty of questions still but from what I have heard so far I do like the sound of this opportunity and I feel sure you and I would work well together. Tell me how do you feel and what might the next steps be?'*

Or perhaps:

> *'I like this organisation and have yet to hear anything that turns me off. I have a little more diligence to do but would like to progress. Do you feel the same way?'*

Or less directly: you might recall the TV detective Columbo. He would question suspects at length but always save his killer question until the meeting had closed. He would be halfway out the door, then swing round and say: 'Oh yeah. Just before I go there was one final thing that I wanted to check with you ...' Caught off guard and thinking they had got away without having to go down this or that particular avenue, he would often gather critical insights from suspects that helped him solve the cases.

In the same way you might have found that just as business meetings draw to a close there is indeed a kind of 'off-the-record moment' that sits outside the meeting proper in which you can learn some critical information. The same applies to interviews. The notebooks close, you both stand up. Now is the time to explore where this goes from here in a manner that suits you.

Try a few approaches out on your friend. Again have a little fun exploring how you can gain wonderful insight with the 'Columbo close'.

Your prompt sheets could probably use an edit and reprint as a result of all that you have learnt in this first role-play session. Make sure you add back in the necessary highlights to help steer your eye and ensure you are as efficiently prompted as possible. Pick out any features and achievements that your friend failed to recall in red. How might you enhance these points to deliver them more convincingly next time?

On your second attempt at Phase 2 try to keep everything as it was on your first run, but put in an additional layer of detail to help your friend really focus on the key criteria you would nail yourself on if you were the interviewer.

By not introducing other variables (such as a new interviewer or different location) you will help keep the focus on the content and delivery, which are what we are looking at here. You will be surprised how much more thorough your interviewer becomes this time around. Now that they have a good feel for the scene and their lines they will be able to give you the grilling you need and that your interview preparation is built to withstand.

🕐 Again keep an eye on the clock.

📖 Take notes on all of their feedback.

Edit your prompt sheets one last time to incorporate any final refinements. These are the small additional touches that can help add that final shine to your performance. Print them off and place them in your interview pack with your CV.

Buy your interviewer a drink and toast yourselves. Well done!

CONFIDENCE

Now you have the confidence and preparedness to see through interviews in a way you will find quite surprising at first. You will be able to set the pace, tone and course of the meeting. You won't have to sweat about how to handle questions and you will have the time to sit back and really study the human being(s) opposite you; to read those small and yet crucial signals their body language gives off.

- Are they really interested in me?
- Did they like that question?
- Are they engaged by this line of enquiry?
- Are we just going through the motions on this one?
- Why the lack of eye contact?
- Are they just playing the cold fish?

You will have the spare capacity to ask yourself these questions through the course of the meeting and your intuition will tell you the answers. You can try appropriate moves throughout the meeting to lead up to your Question 11, your vision question, where you wear your dreams on your sleeve.

Now you really are ready to nail that interview.

WHAT CAN GO WRONG?

It's worth taking a quick glance over your shoulder at this point at what the unexpected might look like. Since you represent at best half of the meeting population that will attend and we can't legislate for the behaviour of the other half, we have to accept that there is much that can go awry.

Here are two choice examples of real-life whacky interviews that prove the point. I am sure these won't happen to you but these extreme examples should help you appreciate that the unexpected can catch you out. You will be better prepared having acknowledged that regardless of how well rehearsed you are the rest of the cast might be working on an entirely different play! Rest assured these examples are very much the exception rather than the norm.

THE BLACK HOLE

A large investment bank would show a group of potential graduate recruits into a cramped room and tell them to wait. No one would monitor them. There were no refreshments, but visits to the toilet were permitted. The first person to come out of the room to complain or ask what was going on would make the next round (showing initiative and bravery in the line of fire perhaps?), while the rest were told they had failed and were shown out of the building without so much as a coffee or even a 'Thanks for coming in'.

Yes, interviews are crazy meetings, but this 'black hole' sounds horrible and, frankly, cruel. This definitely crosses any reasonable line in my view.

STAGE FRIGHT

Here's the second example, for which thanks to Alison:

> I got called for an interview with a major oil corporation. I did the prep work, obsessed over what I would wear, rehearsed my opening and closing … I was ready.
>
> I was escorted to what seemed like a small theatre with a stage and auditorium seating and everything. The interviewer escorted me to a chair on the stage and had me sit in the single chair that was in the middle of the stage, he turned down all the lights except the stage lights and then he went to sit down in the front row.
>
> I thought that was weird enough but then it got really weird.
>
> A bunch of people filed in a door at the back of the theatre and sat in the upper rows. The lights were in my face so I couldn't really see them, but I could hear them moving and whispering and shuffling papers. I was too young and too stupid to ask what was going on. Needless to say it was a terrible interview.
>
> Afterwards as I was walking out I said to the interviewer, 'That was a pretty unusual interview.'
>
> He said, 'If you work for us you need to be always "on", so we feel it's important to know how candidates will do when they are *literally* in the spotlight.'

Again, I think this is completely unfair and unreasonable. Bit by bit and sometimes lump by lump the interviewer should extract a clear view of the actual person you are, along with a gauge of your relative capability but they don't need to resort to cruelty to get there.

As we have seen, the interview forms part of a selection process so prepare to be patient. Sometimes these processes can be self-defeating, as onerous interrogation can artificially choke candidates to the point where the actual person fails to turn up or more likely does turn up but as a shadow of the real thing.

In my experience it is the weak and inexperienced interviewers who are most likely to try a few tricks as part of this process. They can't seem to help themselves.

I very much doubt that you will be subjected to this type of treatment, but if you are I know you are prepared. Prepared at best to turn the whole thing into what you want it to be and at worst to laugh at the weirdness and take your interview pack onwards and upwards to where I am sure your career is headed.

And once again, I'd like to emphasise that interviews of this nature are very much the exception to the rule.

STEP 10: PRACTICE – KEY POINTS

- Get your interview pack ready.
- Practising and preparing give you confidence.
  - Phase 1: Visualisation and self-appraisal
  - Phase 2: Role play
- The two-phase approach helps by first developing the meeting in your mind then rehearsing what you have learnt in a safe and friendly environment.
- Before leaving the meeting, 'close for next steps' to ensure you get at least a sense of how the meeting went and what comes next.
- You can be reassured that you now truly are ready to nail that interview.

PRACTICAL PREPARATION

Having invested a great deal of time in completing the 10 steps you would be forgiven for feeling slightly disappointed that the interview itself will last for just 60 short minutes. But with this hard work done you are ready to make the most of these precious minutes. You are ready to make them work positively for your career.

TRUST IN YOUR PREPARATION

You *are* and *will be* prepared for any interview you attend. However, as I have said previously, we find all too often that you can't say the same for the interviewers that you are destined to meet.

In fact we can be fairly sure that they will be distinctly unprepared. They will likely be relying on the good old 'seat-of-their-pants method' to make up the meeting on the fly: 'I'll know the right candidate when I meet them.' They probably won't take detailed notes, probably won't run any form of structured selection processes and, yes, they will probably forget the various candidates who make up shortlists and need reminding about them.

IT'S IN THE PRESENTATION

You are equipped to present yourself in the best possible light. Imagine for a moment that you have a talent for pottery. You make a collection of really nice pots and you want to sell them. You could put them on eBay, but since you happen to know the owners of Harrods, they offer to give your pots pride of place in a prime window.

Consider the eye of the beholder who gazes in through the Harrods window. What value the pots? Considerably higher than the pots would attract on eBay, that's for sure.

Nail That Interview is the perfect shop window for you. It's your presentation system for *you*. You are the product. In this book we haven't set about altering the product, rather we have worked hard on how best to present the FAB – features, achievements and benefits of this wonderful person so that those who really *should* buy you *do* buy you!

Your thorough preparation and the interviewer's probable lack of any, affords you a commanding position in the meeting, but be prepared to be a little disappointed that they might not seem to be taking it quite as seriously as you. You have no control over how they prepare to interview you so don't let that trouble you.

I assure you that you are well enough prepared for both sides of the meeting and can ensure that the encounter works effectively for the interviewer and you.

NAIL THE BASICS

The waiting can be worse than the event itself, so you might prefer to keep yourself busy prior to the interview.

Relax as best you can. Focus on another project. Immerse yourself in your work. Get into a good book that takes you out of yourself, watch a movie or two. You have reached the point of readiness and no amount of anxiety, worry or stress is going to improve or enhance your performance. On the contrary, fretting will sap your energy and weaken your confidence.

Rest. Gather your energies. The evening before your meeting put your interview pack away and occupy your mind with other things. Don't worry, you are ready to go. As you travel to the interview a glance through the pack's contents is all you will need to reassure you that you can look forward to the meeting with confidence.

PRE-INTERVIEW CHECKS

I hesitate to stress some of the blindingly obvious pre-interview checks that you should carry out, but attending interviews is not part of your normal routine and it's a fact that when we are operating outside of our comfort zone we can switch off to the obvious and find ourselves forgetting what we usually take for granted. So please do bear with me as we plumb the depths of the blindingly obvious.

I happen to be one of those people who likes making to-do lists. I recommend that you make one now of these checks and chores, then tick them off one by one as you complete them.

1. **Logistics** Check and reconfirm the time, the location and the name of the interviewer you are meeting. Have you got their direct line if you need to reach them on the day?
2. **Time off** See if you can book a day or ideally half a day as holiday to allow you time either side of the interview to really focus on your performance.
3. **News and views** Search for the latest news or announcements from the company and their immediate competitors.
4. **Stake-out** Check the street scene on Google Earth. Is it obvious which building it is?
5. **Book travel** Check that your travel plans get you there with plenty of time to spare. You *cannot* be late under any circumstances. Set a secondary alarm on your phone or laptop to remind you to leave in time to catch any necessary transport or to walk. Buy any tickets that you might need in advance.
6. **Decide on your outfit** Choose what clothes you are going to wear. Make sure that your clothes are clean and ironed and your shoes are shined. For corporate roles I would recommend you always wear a suit or formal business attire.

If you are fortunate to work in one of the sectors where smart-casual dress is the norm, then err on the smart side of casual. The interview is not the time to push the boundaries of fashion – unless of course you are a fashion designer, in which case you don't need my advice on what to wear!

7. **Check weather forecast** If rain threatens make sure you put an umbrella by your clothes so that you don't forget to take it with you.

8. **Packing** Double-check your interview pack to make sure it contains:
   - Two clean copies of your CV
   - Prompt Sheet #1 – your stories
   - Prompt Sheet #2 – your nail questions

   Put the pack in the case or bag you will take with you and put it by your clothes. Make sure you have your wallet or purse. Also check that you have a pen, your journal, some business cards if you have them and some notepaper. Make sure that your mobile phone is fully charged and that you have pre-entered the telephone number for the company you are heading to along with the direct line or mobile number of the interviewer or their secretary (in case you get held up). Remember to switch your phone to silent mode before you go into the building.

9. **Sharpen up** Visit the hairdresser for a cut and blow-dry.

HOW DO YOU SMELL?

Sorry to be blunt and personal but this has to be said.

- **Breath** You can't smell your own breath. Halitosis can be brought on by the little extra stress that you might experience on the day of your interview and surveys have regularly shown that bad breath produces a powerful negative sentiment in both men and women. So give your teeth an extra brush, maybe have a good rinse with some mouthwash and keep something minty in your pocket that you can chew just prior to the interview.
- **Scent** I advise you not to use anything except a good underarm deodorant on interview day. I can recall several aftershave-drenched candidates being astonished that I had the temerity to point out that most interviewers might actually prefer to breathe fresh air.

PRACTICAL PREPARATION – KEY POINTS

- Relax! You are far better prepared than your interviewer; however, don't sit and do nothing in the days before your interview or you'll fret. It is important that you do whatever you can to gain and maintain the right attitude.
- Nail the basics – get the practical preparations sorted.

AFTER THE INTERVIEW

Pat yourself on the back for your performance.

I don't care how you feel you did. Really I don't. Every performance can be improved upon and enhanced; every meeting is a learning and development opportunity. By all means wallow in the feeling of euphoria if things went swimmingly or conversely be a harsh critic (both healthy when balanced with each other!), but first recognise that you have taken a huge step forwards by walking through the interview doorway.

Well done!

SEND A HARD-COPY FOLLOW-UP

You need to remind the interviewer how good you are.

Following your interview there could well have been any number of events crop up that served to drown the good, positive feelings that the interviewer felt as you shook hands and parted. These positive feelings are easily resuscitated 24 to 48 hours after the interview with a note to follow up.

In terms of what you should write, I have set out some of the key themes in the table below that will help you formulate your note. Develop a message using your own style but try to incorporate the content listed here.

It's fine to email the note, but actually printed hard copy sent in the post is best for this type of important communication.

Content guide for interview follow-up letter		
Theme	Meaning/Sentiment	Purpose/Outcome
Appreciation – Respect	Thank you.	Good manners.
Recollection – Reminder	Particularly engaged by your thinking on ... ... well aligned with my own feeling/thinking I felt.	Interviewer will think: 'Aha, I recall we laughed at that. Yes, this candidate is the one who knew our clients had been challenged by that issue ...'
I like you and the opportunity	Would relish the possibility of working with you ... Am inspired by where the business is today and the vision you paint from here.	People like people who like them. People like people who make them feel proud of their own situation.
Next steps	You mentioned I should hear from you next week and to call if I had any queries in the meantime. I have many further questions but they will hold until we meet. I look forward to being given the opportunity to ...	Be bold and assumptive. If you lose a deal you ask for you were never going to get it. If you lose one because you didn't ask – you'll never know!

YOUR INTERVIEW RECOLLECTIONS

 As soon as possible record your recollections of the meeting. Perhaps you can do this in a café around the corner after the interview or as you're travelling home. Note down your thoughts while they are fresh in your mind. This is where your journal becomes a record that captures your career insights as you travel your career journey.

I cannot overstress the value of capturing these priceless insights into yourself and your career. If you do this, your journal will soon contain a collection of all the clues that will help you open the doors to your future.

What you write is entirely up to you, but I would encourage you to write down whatever is in your mind. Just scribble down everything that occurs to you. Here is a mixed bag of the sort of thoughts some of our candidates have shared straight after leaving the meeting:

- 'My nerves were quickly settled by his calm and reassuring approach … coffee was revolting though!'
- 'I only got four of my prompt questions out. She was a big talker and actually didn't really grill me at all. However, what she did ask were a lot of questions about what makes me tick and what I do outside of work.'
- 'There was a notable pause from her when we got on to last year's performance. I wasn't sure she entirely bought my message about how we achieved it. But the moment passed.'
- 'He was very unclear on next steps. Actually I got the impression he really didn't know what happened next.'
- 'He pretty much offered me the job. Then he caught himself and described the usual spiel about process blah blah!'

INTERVIEW DEBRIEF

The questions we use to debrief candidates might prove helpful when recording your recollections.

- How did it go?
- How long were you there?
- Did you get along (with the interviewer on a personal level)?
- What did you talk about in general?
- How many of your nail questions did you deliver? *Rate those you did deliver for effectiveness.*
- How many of your prompt stories did you tell? *Rate those you did deliver for effectiveness.*

- How was the position described to you?
- Were you introduced to/interviewed by anyone else?
- Was a second interview set or discussed?
- Did the subject of money come up? *If so what was discussed?*
- What kind of future can you see for yourself at this company?
- Did you ask your vision question? *How did they respond?*
- Is there anything that would prevent you from accepting an offer at this time?
- How did you leave it with them?
- What is it going to take for you to accept an offer from this company?

From these reflections a set of outstanding questions that remain to be answered should also emerge. Make a note of these ready for your next interview in the process. Get ready to deliver your next performance be it part of this process or another one.

FEEDBACK

Honest feedback is often difficult to get, unless of course it is overwhelmingly positive, in which case you will tend to get a gushing 'Yes!' Even then the interviewer will probably gloss over any concerns they picked up in the interview, so actually you are getting only selected sound bites as opposed to anything truly constructive.

Don't settle for anything less than full feedback. Warts and all. Recruiters, where you work with them, should help tease out the details for you. However, if all else fails you should call or write to the interviewer directly and simply ask for honest and frank feedback. You may well have to read through lots of HR-speak to pick out the weak points (there is plenty of legislation they need to step around in hiring), but all feedback is valuable.

What you learn from an interview meeting will fuel all those that follow, so try to draw as much from each meeting as you can.

*

The more interviews you attend the more you will come to revel in where these meetings can take you and your career. Each new height you scale will reveal yet more possibilities. Each time you set out to climb the interview mountain you have a 10-step plan that makes you sure of your footing.

The enthusiasm success breeds is a powerful drug that further fuels your momentum. With your hands firmly on the controls of your career, you will relish the interview staging posts ahead.

AFTER THE INTERVIEW – KEY POINTS

- Pat yourself on the back.
- Write to your interviewer (preferably a hard-copy letter) to remind them how good you are.
- Capture your thoughts about the meeting in your journal as soon as you can after it has finished.
- Ask for constructive feedback.

YOU ARE READY TO NAIL THAT INTERVIEW

You are ready. You feel ready. You enjoy self-awareness such as the vast majority of candidates never attain. You have an attitude you can and will wear proudly, one of assured yet measured confidence. And remember that your attitude is what interviewers actually hire.

What role they hire you for becomes a central question for the interviewer when you apply all that you have learnt here. You enter the meeting equipped to help the interviewer explore well beyond the bounds of the obvious question:

Do I like this candidate for the job they are interviewing for?

You will be pressing them to consider:

How best can I help this candidate get a strong foothold here in our company so that they can help me and my colleagues meet our personal and company goals?

There is and always will be a school of thought that maintains that good candidates should just 'line up and be counted'. In this school the interview meeting belongs to the interviewer who is the ultimate decision maker. Such sentiments I recognise and respect because they are deeply entrenched but the title of this book is *Nail That Interview*. Not *Do Okay*, *Do Fine* or *Do All Right in Interviews* but *Nail That Interview*!

You and I know that this is *your* meeting. You are going to hold your head high above the parapet of the normal, mediocre, run-of-the-mill employees out there and ask the world to help you find the role of your dreams.

The interview is the open doorway through which you pass from one phase of your career to another. From now on, as you knock on each door to ask your interviewer to let you through, you will first and foremost be true to yourself. You have, through the 10 steps completed here, got to know yourself better than the vast majority of working professionals ever get to know themselves.

Now comes the distillation of that knowledge into the delivery phase, as you go into these great meetings.

You can choose whether or not to pass through the door, but you know now that regardless you will gain priceless insight from all the interviewers you meet.

Never again will you interview for a job, rather you will from now on *nail that interview* to accelerate you along your career journey.

Hold tight and enjoy the ride.

INDEX